WOMEN WORLD LEADERS PRESENTS

UNSEEN
YOU ARE NOT ALONE

VISIONARY AUTHORS
MENDEZ NELSON & LISA TOFANO HATHAWAY

Table of Contents

Introduction

God sees you where you are right now. In fact, He knew you would be holding this book at this very moment—He orchestrated it.

Holy and mighty God, the King of kings and Lord of the universe, longs to speak to *you*. He wants to tell you that you are not alone or forgotten—He is always with you. Your heavenly Father is compassionately drawing you into His arms. He loves you just as you are; no performance or pretending is needed. You can come to Him as you are. It's not necessary for you to hide anything—He already sees and knows it all anyway. *Trust in him at all times, you people; pour out your hearts to him, for our God is our refuge* (Psalm 62:8 NIV).

God designed us to need others—so why are our relationships such a struggle? And why, even when there are so many others around us, do we all experience times when we feel lonely, invisible, and unseen? How can we experience feelings of disconnection and intense loneliness in the middle of a crowd? Why are there times when we seem so utterly abandoned and alone?

We all desire love, acceptance, and community, yet we struggle with knowing how to get those needs met. There are so many avenues designed to provide us with connection—social media outlets, school clubs, community organizations—but we still often feel unnoticed. The connections we long for can seem impossible to grasp. While everyone else's lives look perfect and full, and though ours may appear that way to the outside world, inwardly, we fight feelings of emptiness and loneliness. There are times we can't help seeing ourselves as overlooked or even insignificant.

We wrote this book to tell you that your feelings are real. We understand them—because we have struggled, too. But we also have good news to share with you that can transform your life and change your perspective of who you are.

You see, although God designed you to need others, He is also a jealous God who wants your most intimate relationship to be with Him. God is ready and willing to meet you where you are. Just because we may *feel* as if we are alone doesn't mean we are. It means we are human. Our emotions can trick us into believing lies that we are abandoned or unworthy instead of trusting that what God says is true: that you are His prized masterpiece whom He cherishes and cares for. The good news is that we can learn to rely on what God says instead of how we feel. Our feelings will rise and fall, but God—who He is and how much He loves you—never changes.

Even when you feel disregarded and forgotten by the world, know that you are significant to God! He sees you and is pursuing you! Our loving heavenly Father is the Good Shepherd who leaves the 99 to search for the one sheep who has gone astray. And when He finds you, He is overwhelmed with joy as He gathers you in His arms. Jesus Himself shared this with us, saying, *"And when he [the shepherd] finds it [the one wandering sheep], he joyfully puts it on his shoulders and goes home. Then he calls his friends and neighbors together and says, 'Rejoice with me; I have found my lost sheep'"* (Luke 15:5-6 NIV).

As a visionary author for *Unseen: You Are Not Alone,* I was inspired to begin this project when three college students contacted me in the same week with the same exact issue—even though they were surrounded daily by many people, they felt completely invisible, totally disconnected, and utterly alone.

The contributing authors in this unique book have openly and honestly shared their personal struggles of feeling isolated and unnoticed, but that isn't the end of their stories. Each one tells how God helped her overcome her struggle and find the one thing that truly matters: God Himself. Their stories, along with the devotional teachings between the chapters, shed light on God's truth and dispel the lies of the darkness. The truth is we are always seen by God, even when we are unnoticed by the world. In Him, we are never alone!

Scripture is full of examples of God letting ordinary people know He saw them. Hagar, Nathanael, Zaccheus, the woman at the well, and the shepherds in the field the night Jesus was born are just a few. Like them, as we *"Behold the Lamb of God, who takes away the sin of the world,"* as the Bible says in John 1:29 (ESV), we are transformed. When we accept Him as our Savior, our inner nature changes. *Therefore, if any man be in Christ, he is a new creature: old things are passed away; behold, all things are become new* (2 Corinthians 5:17 KJV).

God knew from the beginning we would need a Savior. Sin separated us from Him, so He sent His only Son, Jesus, into the world to die in our place to pay the penalty for our sin. If you declare with your mouth, *"Jesus is Lord,"* and believe in your heart that God raised him from the dead, you will be saved. For it is with your heart that you believe and are justified, and it is *with your mouth that you profess your faith and are saved* (Romans 10:9-10 NIV). If you have not yet received the Lord Jesus as your Savior, as you read, be open to His call. God's desire, and our desire, is for you to come to know Jesus personally as your Savior and Lord. Your first step is to ask God to help you trust and receive Him.

We know the stories in this book will give you a new perspective on why you feel abandoned and alone. They will illuminate that God is ready and willing to help you with these emotions if you offer them to Him. As we tell our stories, we hope you will reflect on yours and recall what God has done, is doing, and will do for you. And we pray you will hear God's voice and be inspired to seek His truth as you let His light shine on the dark lies in your mind, setting you free from their grip. As you read, may you sense God's presence with you, and may you experience him as El Roi, "The God Who Sees Me."

We have referenced scripture throughout. In each case, we have given the book of the Bible where the passage can be found, followed by the chapter and verse. For example, John 3:16 denotes that the verse comes from the book of John, chapter three, verse 16. If you see an a or b after the verse, that simply refers to which part of the verse is being quoted. (Lowercase a is the first half of the verse; lowercase b is the second half or last part of the verse.) Additionally, many different versions of the Bible are used throughout this book. You will see them as uppercase letters after the Scripture reference, such as NIV (New International Version), ESV (English Standard Version), and NKJV (New King James Version). A full listing of each version used with its abbreviation is found on the front copyright page.

On behalf of all the authors of *Unseen: You Are Not Alone,* thank you for embarking on this journey with us. We have prayed for you. We appreciate you. And we know God will bless you through what He has prompted us to share. May the Holy Spirit work within you, inspiring you to become aware of how God has worked in your past, is working in your present, and will work in your future circumstances. You are never alone. He sees you.

I will instruct you and teach you in the way you should go; I will counsel you with my loving eye on you (Psalm 32:8 NIV).

MENDEZ NELSON

Mendez Nelson is an Occupational Therapist. She lives in Madison, Mississippi. Her husband, Kevin, is an Oral Oncology Dentist. They attend Fondren Church.

Mendez is on the Magnolia Speech School Board. She serves as Board Secretary for the Crisis Pregnancy Center of Southwest Mississippi. She also serves on the Mississippi Occupational Therapy Association Board as Legislative Co-Chair of the Mental Health Committee. Additionally, Mendez volunteers as a committee member with Anchored: A Christian Grief Retreat to help young girls and teens cope with the loss of loved ones. Finally, she serves on Emmaus and Chrysalis Retreat Teams.

Mendez felt called to initiate the writing of this book so readers would know they are loved and seen by God. Her prayer is that as you read the chapters and teaching-devotions in *Unseen,* you will sense God's presence and know that you are always seen by Him.

Coming Out of the Dark Shadows of Shame

by Mendez Nelson

> *God is light; in him there is no darkness at all* (1 John 1:5b NIV).

"You are hateful, no one likes you, and you don't have any friends." I vividly remember these words being said to me when I was a young child. They haunted me into adulthood. These painful words played over and over on repeat in my mind. I was told this by a trusted adult, so naturally, I believed them to be true. As a result, I withdrew and isolated myself from others. Shameful thoughts took over my mind: *I am not like everyone else. Something is wrong with me. I'm not even likable.* The shameful thoughts cascaded in constantly like a powerful waterfall. *No one cares about me. I don't matter. God must feel this way about me, too.*

Unhealthy thought patterns emerged as dark, shameful thoughts overtook me. I began to feel as if I was in some sort of glass room where I could see out, but no one could see inside. I wished I could talk to someone about this, but I knew no one cared because they didn't like me. I was all alone.

Scared. Sad. Shamed. Unseen.

Shame is like a dark cloud that overshadows our minds. It makes us think we are unlovable and disconnects us from others. The Bible tells us that God's grace, wisdom, and love are multifaceted and are intended for good. I believe shame is also multifaceted, with many different dark sides and hidden layers. It causes fear, doubt, discouragement, and depression. Shame is not good and is not from God. It is not intended for our good.

One biblical definition of shame is simply "scornful whisperings." I began to hear nonstop whisperings of scorn the very instant I believed the lie I had been told. Lies are powerful only if we think they are true. I accepted that statement as truth because it was said to me at an early age by an adult I loved, trusted, and admired.

As a result, I began to develop unhealthy coping skills. Desperately wanting people to like me and wanting so badly to have friends, I tried really hard to do all the things I thought were necessary to be loved and accepted. Even at that young age, something inside me longed for close community, but knowing people didn't like me, I didn't know how to go about having relationships. So, I became a people pleaser. In my young mind, I thought, *Surely, people will like me if I do things for them they want.*

God's Word plainly tells us not to live to please others or ourselves; instead, we are to aim to please Him alone. His Word tells us to pour out our hearts to Him and come to Him with our burdens. Instead, I kept the weight of the world on my own shoulders. I believed God loved everyone except me. I was unlovable. I had to accept this, so I tried to be independent, strong, and self-sufficient. Living this way was very isolating. I always had to project a happy, problem-free existence even though I was living with more afflictions than the average person my age likely had. I became fixated on pleasing others and trying to fix other people's problems since there obviously was no solution for my own.

I grew up attending church and memorizing Bible verses, so I knew what God's Word said. Yet, somehow, I thought people who believed in God were supposed to always be happy and never have problems. This wrong belief caused me a lot of unnecessary pain and suffering. I was sure other people must've known that God didn't love me. I constantly wrestled inwardly with thoughts and feelings, but outwardly, I pretended to have it all together. I learned to stuff my true feelings deep inside as I began to feel completely insignificant and invisible.

Because I wanted to be liked and valued, my image—how things appeared to others—was what I believed mattered the most, so I focused on the exterior landscape while the interior became darker and darker. I began to be seen as someone who was always happy and never had any problems. People assumed I was mature and had life figured out, so they began to come to me with their problems. I performed to meet other people's expectations.

Internally, I felt a great deal of despair and hopelessness. *If God and other people would only like me, I wouldn't have to think like this and live this way.* I grew angry. The shadows of shame had caused such intense darkness in my heart and mind that it had totally eclipsed the light of Christ from my view. On top of that, fear and shame kept me from letting other people know who I really was.

My focus shifted back and forth—from blaming God to blaming myself and others for my darkness. In my mind, I knew that God's light was not fully shining on me, and I had to hold someone responsible. I was so blinded that I couldn't see that it was my own choice to believe the lies that actually were keeping me in the bondage of the enemy's strongholds.

Our suffering in the darkness makes us feel unseen, especially if we believe

God caused it or another person is to blame for it. I spent a great deal of time blaming myself, others, and even God for the haunting thoughts. God's Word assures us that He is with us in our adversities, including those we create ourselves. He does not abandon us when we make wrong choices based on erroneous beliefs. God's Holy Spirit continuously points us to grace and truth.

At my darkest, I recalled the one person who always showed me uncondi-tional love. Her skin was so thin it was almost transparent. You could see her veins; they looked like blue spider webs. Blood thinners caused dark spots of bruising all over her arms. She had too many wrinkles to count. She could no longer stand up straight and used a walker to get around. She didn't wear makeup, but she was absolutely the most beautiful woman I had ever seen. The love of God poured out from her. His light radiated from her smile. Joy danced in her sparkling eyes. She was my memaw, and she loved me. She called me darling. She saw into my soul. I couldn't lie to her by saying I was fine if I wasn't. She knew. God sent her into my life to make me feel seen and unashamed. We spent as much time together as possible. She made me feel unconditionally loved and accepted. Memaw always wanted to know how I was doing and what was going on in my life. She would ask me how I was feeling. Honestly, I hated her asking me that because I never knew how to answer. I did not know how I felt. I did not know how to feel. I only knew how to be numb. I did not know how to open up and share my feelings, even with the one person who always showed me unconditional love without judgment.

Do you recall how big and scary shadows appeared to be when we were children? Our imaginations would run wild with fear over all the possible scenarios of what was lurking in the darkness. But the enormous spooky shadows would suddenly vanish when we turned on the light. What a relief! Thankfully, we could see they were really nothing at all. Research about shadows shows that when something is close to the origin of the light, it will block out more light, making the shadow appear big even though the object casting the shadow is actually very small. This is a huge revelation! It means we need to be closer to the source of the light so that our enemy cannot come between us with his scary, evil blackness.

Shame causes these shadows of fear to eclipse our hearts, minds, and thoughts. When emotions are suppressed long enough, they numb us, and then we begin to accept lies such as our feelings don't matter anyway. Our self-worth hits rock bottom and causes us to become a doormat to meet others' expectations at all times and at all costs while we ignore our own needs. Complete and utter isolation, along with extreme fatigue and exhaustion, are the results. We also face the possibility of developing relationships with people who only call when they need us to do something for them—people who don't give; they just take.

At one point in my life, I allowed myself to be a doormat. Ironically, I developed an exaggerated sense of self-importance because so many people needed me for so many things. It felt like a win for me. I was successful at pleasing people. I finally felt as if I was liked, loved, and accepted. I made myself totally available at all times. I had zero healthy boundaries. I was an enabler and had become completely co-dependent. It never occurred to me to consider how choosing to live this way made me feel or how unequal most of my relationships were. Actually, I didn't even realize I had a choice; I just thought, *this is what I must do to get people to like and accept me.* I ignored my feelings, needs, and desires, ultimately making me feel totally invisible. I began to feel good only when I took on things I wasn't responsible for to help others. I forcefully bulldozed myself into complying with others' desires while ignoring my own. My internal suffering was my fault for not establishing healthy boundaries. I had not allowed others in too close because I didn't want them to see how fragile I really was. Plus, if they knew the real me, they wouldn't like me. At least by giving others what they wanted, I had friends.

I even pretended to be strong and unbreakable through my parent's divorce, my brother's suicide, being unable to have children, and becoming a widow. This was not fun or easy, but I had never lived any other way. I did not know how to express my true feelings. I felt as if I would fall apart if I opened up to anyone. Plus, I did not want to put undue burdens on others. Truthfully, I was hoping somehow, someone would see past the façade and administer relief for my unbearable pain.

People cannot help you when you act as if everything is okay and nothing is wrong. We are supposed to turn to God when we need help. I had become so independent and self-sufficient that I began to believe the lie that even God couldn't see me, so how could He help me? I could not envision any good in my past, present, or future. I felt further isolated because I believed I was the only person in the world having to uphold an image and suppress feelings while putting on a front that I had it all under control.

Pretending things are perfect is not the way God designed us to live. It surely does not promote peace. We can fake happiness, but we cannot fake peace. True peace cannot be manufactured; it only comes from God. He alone is the only source of real and lasting peace. God created us for community and fellowship with Him and with each other so we can reflect His glory in this dark world.

But if we walk in the light, as he is in the light, we have fellowship with one another, and the blood of Jesus, his Son, purifies us from all sin (1 John 1:7 NIV).

Our heavenly Father knows we are not perfect and has never expected us to be. I thought maybe if I could portray the illusion of perfection in having it all together, I could maintain the relationships that I had worked so hard to get.

> *But he said to me, "My grace is sufficient for you, for my power is made perfect in weakness"* (2 Corinthians 12:9 NIV).

For as long as I can remember, there has been a vicious cycle of shame inside my head. I had developed a pattern in my mind of negative thinking about myself. I was never able to see anything good in me. I had not one positive thought about myself. Anxiety woke me up every morning and kept me from falling asleep at night. I tried to ignore it as I had always done with everything else I felt, but it only grew louder. Fear, guilt, shame, and condemnation accompanied my anxious thoughts. But it all subsided when I came to know Christ as my Savior.

I became born again at the age of thirty, and everything changed. I began to saturate my mind with the truth of God's Word. This helped to dispel the lies I was believing. Light began to fill my mind. The shadows of shame were shrinking. I began to see God at work in my life and learned that He saw me, too.

> *The light shines in the darkness, and the darkness has not overcome it... The true light that gives light to everyone was coming into the world* (John 1:5, 9 NIV).

Not only does God see us, but He sees us as a light for Him. And He wants others to see His light in us so they will be drawn to Him. Believing the truth instead of lies gave me freedom. I no longer felt invisible, insignificant, and unseen. I actually even began to feel loved and accepted by God and others. This enabled me to develop healthy friendships with other Christians.

Things don't become perfect when we get saved. Actually, the opposite is true. We become free from trying to have to pretend we are perfect. This freedom was such a welcomed relief for me.

No matter who we are, there will be times we spend in the valley as well as times we spend on the mountaintop. This is because we have an enemy who came with the purpose of stealing, killing, and destroying, but our Savior came with the purpose of giving us abundant life, even in the midst of the trials we encounter in this dark world. We can learn to walk by faith and not by sight, but not by our own feelings or our own understanding.

We can learn to walk through difficult times while maintaining peace by managing our thoughts and fixing them on the Lord no matter what comes against us. We are not equipped to walk through this life on our own, but with help from the Lord, we can find joy even in the hard times.

Jesus told us, *"You are the light of the world. A town built on a hill cannot be hidden...In the same way, let your light shine before others, that they may see your good deeds and glorify your Father in heaven"* (Matthew 5:14, 16 NIV).

The light of Christ is given to us by God to enable us to see what He is doing in and around us.

I keep asking that the God of our Lord Jesus Christ, the glorious Father, may give you the Spirit of wisdom and revelation, so that you may know him better. I pray that the eyes of your heart may be enlightened in order that you may know the hope to which he has called you, the riches of his glorious inheritance in his holy people, and his incomparably great power for us who believe (Ephesians 1:17-19a NIV).

Deep down, we all yearn to be truly seen. We all have some level of desire for acceptance, attention, affection, affirmation, and admiration. Most of us try to get these needs met in all the wrong ways. God alone is the one and only source of true fulfillment of our innermost longings. He knows us completely, and He is always there for us.

Where can I go from your Spirit?
Where can I flee from your presence?
If I go up to the heavens, you are there;
if I make my bed in the depths, you are there.
If I rise on the wings of the dawn,
if I settle on the far side of the sea,
even there your hand will guide me,
your right hand will hold me fast.
If I say, "Surely the darkness will hide me
and the light become night around me,"
even the darkness will not be dark to you;
the night will shine like the day,
for darkness is as light to you.

For you created my inmost being;
you knit me together in my mother's womb.
I praise you because I am fearfully and wonderfully made;
your works are wonderful,
I know that full well.
My frame was not hidden from you
when I was made in the secret place,
when I was woven together in the depths of the earth.
Your eyes saw my unformed body;
all the days ordained for me were written in your book
before one of them came to be.
(Psalm 139:7-16 NIV)

God loves us. He sees and hears all our cries and sighs and tears and desires. He wants to heal the brokenness and hurts caused by living in this dark world. The enemy sends people into our lives to make us feel shame, but God sends people into our lives to help us feel seen. The only way to feel seen is to let the light of Christ shine on you. The truth of His Word will show you how loved and valued you are.

By welcoming God into my life, He has done all this and more for me. I am no longer a widow. God sent an incredible man into my life. He makes me feel seen, valued, and loved. God has also sent me a community of friends who see me and love me for who I am. And by studying His Word, God constantly reminds me that because I am His daughter, I am enough. I am now living free and believing truth.

So can you. You are never alone. You are always seen.

You Are Not Alone in Shame

by Mendez Nelson

Do you have trouble putting a finger on what you are wrestling with? Could it be anxiety, fear, deception, or condemnation? How about shame? Does that word resonate deep inside your soul? Why do we wrestle with thoughts and feelings of shame? And where do they come from?

Our flesh is the part of us that Jesus tells us to die to and crucify daily. It is the part of our inner self that rebels against God. It is the part of us that exposes us to shame. Romans 8:5-8 NIV explains it this way: *Those who live according to the flesh have their minds set on what the flesh desires; but those who live in accordance with the Spirit have their minds set on what the Spirit desires. The mind governed by the flesh is death, but the mind governed by the Spirit is life and peace. The mind governed by the flesh is hostile to God; it does not submit to God's law, nor can it do so. Those who are in the realm of the flesh cannot please God* (NIV).

Our loving heavenly Father does not want us to live a life of shame. In fact, when He created Adam and Eve in the Garden of Eden, His Word tells us in Genesis 2:25b (NIV), *They felt no shame.* It wasn't until sin came into the world as a result of their disobedience that shame was able to enter into their existence.

Sadly, shame is a huge epidemic plaguing our world today. It is certainly not from God. Shame is from the enemy of our souls. He uses it as a stronghold to keep us bound, imprisoned, and disconnected from others. God created us to live in freedom and harmony. He does not want us to experience shame or isolation. In the animal kingdom, predators look for the weakest creature to strike unexpectedly. They target it, isolate it from the others, and then launch their attack on it. Our enemy works in much the same way. He attacks our minds with shame in an attempt to isolate and defeat us so we will give up entirely.

> *Your enemy the devil prowls around like a roaring lion looking for someone to devour* (1 Peter 5:8b NIV).

One biblical meaning of shame is "disgrace." God covers us with His grace; the enemy wants to cover us with disgrace. Grace connects us, while disgrace separates us. Likewise, God's grace encourages us, while shame and disgrace discourage us. When we are guilty of sin, God's Holy Spirit gently convicts us while our enemy assaults us with condemnation and accusations. Condemnation is not from God.

> *Therefore, there is now no condemnation for those who are in Christ Jesus, because through Christ Jesus the law of the Spirit who gives life has set you free from the law of sin and death* (Romans 8:1-2 NIV).

Shame is rooted in fear. God's perfect love drives out fear. God does not want His children to live in fear; He desires for us to live in freedom. He tells us plainly through the writings of Paul in Galatians 5:1 (NIV), *It is for freedom that Christ has set us free. Stand firm, then, and do not let yourselves be burdened again by a yoke of slavery.*

In order to live free from shame, we must know the truth and learn to hear God's voice. The voice of shame is not from God. Do not listen to it. Our heavenly Father loves us, sees us, and longs to speak to us. We must cultivate the skill of tuning out all voices that are not His. As God's children, His sheep, we can hear His voice when He speaks to us. Jesus said, *"My sheep listen to my voice; I know them, and they follow me"* (John 10:27 NIV).

Jesus never condemns or shames anyone. He always shows love, grace, mercy, and forgiveness. God's goodness and mercy follow us all the days of our lives. Shame no longer has a place in our lives as believers. Let's start living shamelessly free for Christ today!

. . . .

LISA TOFANO HATHAWAY

Lisa Tofano Hathaway is a lover of Jesus who has a passion for the least of these. Her heartbeat is to see those who need a second chance experience the tangible love of Jesus. She has learned to worship through suffering as a special needs mom, recent breast cancer survivor, and survivor of a tragic car accident within a two-year time span. Suffering has been intertwined in her story, and she wants others to experience the sweetness of God through some of the most difficult things in life. She comes alive when others experience the redemptive love of Jesus.

Lisa resides in Lexington, NC, with her amazing husband of 22 years, Everett, and her precious children, Savannah, Andrew, and Luke. She loves family and pouring love into others.

She has an MBA and through the adversities in life, has stepped into God's calling on her life to become a Licensed Clinical Mental Health Counselor. She currently works at The Oaks Therapeutic Community, a Christ-centered counseling and wellness consulting community dedicated to supporting individuals on their journey toward worth and wellness while finding the value God gives each person.

Behind the Scenes

by Lisa Tofano Hathaway

God has an uncanny way of showing us who He is in our struggles and hardships. Through difficult times, He prunes us and grows us into who He wants us to be. Even if the picture-perfect life we dream of as a child is crushed, God continues to see us for who we are and meets us on the journey. God is not a substitution for our earthy fathers—He is perfect beyond what any human could ever be. And there is a space reserved in our hearts that only He can fill. Throughout my life, I have had the opportunity to see God's hand personally and intimately as He has orchestrated everything behind the scenes of my life.

From birth, I spent my entire childhood as a preacher's kid. I was born in Fort Worth, Texas, while my dad was in seminary. My mom, dad, brother, and I all lived in a tiny seminary duplex while my dad finished his degree. After he finished his schooling, we moved around every three years— whenever he was called to other churches to preach. I could not plant roots in any location, which was challenging as a child. Children want to establish friendships, play with next-door neighbors, and celebrate birthdays with their group of friends. My brother and I did not have that. We just went through the motions of moving every three years.

We moved to California and were only there for a year. Then, we moved from California to North Carolina and then back to Texas. I vividly remember attending three different schools during 2nd grade. As I entered each classroom as the "new kid," it grew harder and harder for me. I felt so unseen each time. No one likes to be the "new kid" or deal with all the emotions that come with that. It became the norm to walk into an already established classroom of kids, not knowing anyone. I constantly felt like an outsider—a feeling that would follow me throughout high school.

I had my brother to talk to, but he was two and a half years older than me, and I was so protective of him and how he was fitting in. My focus shifted to making sure he was ok with all these transitions. When I was in 3rd grade, we moved to West Texas, where my dad became a pastor at a church in a very small town. That is where I finally began to develop friendships. I went to the skating rink every weekend and felt like I was starting to "fit in." I felt included and a part of something. Skating became my lifeline, even though I would get grounded from it if I was disobedient to my parents. It was like the end of the world when they would take skating away from me. Little did I know my newfound belonging wouldn't last. Just like the other previous times, we eventually uprooted what little roots had been grown and moved once again. It felt like I was being pulled out of the ground each time we moved.

As we traveled from West Texas to North Carolina, I had a lengthy and thought-filled ride in a U-Haul truck. My twelve-year-old mind was trying to process how my parents could move us at such a difficult age. That drive is still so vivid in my mind. You know, there are those memories that stand out in your mind because of the impact they have on your life. This was one of those times. I had just started to feel "seen" in Texas by my friends there, yet we were being uprooted again. I knew this meant another new school, another adjustment to a new church, a new parsonage, and, hopefully, a fresh start for my parents. There was a significant amount of arguing in the different places we lived, and I was praying that God would give us a fresh start in North Carolina.

I began attending my new school in January of my 6th grade. The kids stared at me as I walked in wearing my black pants, shirt, and Keds. Keds were popular in Texas but not so much in North Carolina. I found that out quickly as the kids stared at me from head to toe. I would soon become the "preacher's kid with an accent from Texas." As I sat at the table with the other students and started talking, my Southern Texas accent was immediately on full display. The kids looked at me like I had arrived from another planet. I felt so out of place; it was hard for me to accept the fact we had left Texas—the place where I had felt like I fit in.

I came home from school and cried to my mom. I felt unseen. I knew this was where our family was to be, but that didn't mean I understood. I was confused. I felt so out of place and uncomfortable. My brother adapted quickly; he was an amazing football player and joined the middle school football team. Sports have a way of bringing instant friends and connections. He quickly became the star football player and won an award in 8th grade as the new student. When we attended the athletic banquet, I recall standing there watching my dad beam with such pride for my brother. You see, my dad lived his life through my brother. Satan has a way of planting seeds in our minds that we are not good enough and can't measure up. This was a pivotal point for me to experience such a foreign place as a new student and navigate the comparison I was feeling toward my brother. I felt like I was always striving for my dad's attention, which followed me for a significant amount of time.

In 8th grade, I began a relationship with a boy that lasted through high school. This was something that, in hindsight, I did not realize would shape me for the rest of my life. He was a stability in my life during one of the most challenging seasons. I began to find my identity in him and our relationship, and I found that dependency grow in the following years. Being a preacher's kid and being forced to move from state to state and city to city was not what I had ever wanted to experience growing up. I was always the "new kid." I've always heard how hard it is to be in a preacher's family; that statement was true for me. When our family moved from Texas to North Carolina, I prayed we would remain for a while so I could start planting roots that would grow.

When I was fifteen, my parents brought my brother and me into their bedroom of the ranch-style parsonage. I knew something didn't feel right in my heart. God has always given me the gift of discernment, and this time, He confirmed it. My parents told us they were separating and would move towards a divorce. I was in shock. How could a pastor of a church get divorced? The questions kept coming. I remember how calm their demeanor was when they told us. My brother and I process things so differently. I cried and cried. It didn't make sense to my fifteen-year-old brain. I was ashamed at that moment that I would be a statistic as a product of divorce. What would everyone in the small town think? How were we going to go to school and face everyone? We were "preacher's kids," and our life was supposed to be perfect, right?

It was a difficult year and years moving forward. I constantly felt I had to mask my feelings to be there for my dad. My brother and I stayed with my mom, but many people turned their backs on him because my dad was a pastor and left the ministry—something that was not popular at all back then. Divorce was more of an obscurity. Families staying together was the norm. I became the person who was constantly there for my dad. The divorce became final when I was sixteen. My brother had just left for college out of state. It felt like I was left to work through everything on my own—as if I was behind the scenes in a nightmare-type movie, navigating my way through.

I knew what this meant with the looming days of the divorce being final in the fall of 1993. The concept of being part of a happy, complete family was broken. It was hard to comprehend this new reality in my life. My parents would more than likely find other partners and remarry. Those thoughts were at the forefront of my mind, but I honestly didn't think they would become a reality.

My parents dated other people, which was so strange to my high school brain. Then, in the spring of my senior year in 1995, my parents chose to remarry other people. I went to both my dad's wedding and my mom's wedding within the span of two weeks. *How in the world could this be happening?* Not only were they getting married, they were doing this in an important year of my life, just before my high school graduation. Many thoughts and feelings that filled my head and heart were not lining up. One particular thought stuck out: just how insignificant I felt. I felt I was holding all the pieces together for my family. I was the one they counted on; I had to grow up fast and learn so much responsibility that was never in my plan.

Honestly, as I look back, even as I type this, those emotions flood back. I remember the dresses I wore to the weddings as I wondered how that could be my reality. I recall asking God why all that was happening. And I knew I would not get the answers I wanted from Him. I knew I was just supposed to trust His plan, even if He dislikes divorce. Everything I thought I knew about life, marriage, and family became unsubstantiated. My parents chose not to work on their marriage as there were other factors involved. Was this what I would remember when and if I ever got married? In my eighteen-year-old head, this would affect me for a long time in all my relationships. My relationship with the guy I dated for seven years ended in my junior of college. I had strived continuously for his love, and I had overlooked the toxic nature of the relationship, feeling I had to in order to be accepted and loved. We can never underestimate the power of watching our parents go through a divorce and the feeling of "not being good enough."

Step-parents, step-siblings, and blended families became my reality. As I walked through this journey, figuring out the pieces was extremely difficult. *I have a dad, but I live with my mom and stepdad.* At eighteen, a time that should have been exciting because I was deciding about college and what I would do with my life, I felt so unseen by my family. The feelings of loneliness overtook me. The on-and-off relationship with the same boyfriend always left me in a place of not being good enough. I found myself striving for his affirmation. But the only one who could truly affirm me was God.

> *Because you are precious in my eyes, and honored, and I love you, I give men in return for you, peoples in exchange for your life* (Isaiah 43:4 ESV).

Many years later, I can now say that walking through all this in my teenage years shaped me in many ways—some positive and some not. Hardships have a way of making our lives better if we choose to let them. I had no idea I would continue through my early twenties and even into my marriage striving for love. Our past has a way of catching up to us, but God is a God of redemption, and He can save us from our past and bring us new life.

I was saved when I was seven years old, but it was in college when I truly saw God in a totally different way. He knows the exact moment in our lives when our eyes need to be opened to His sweetness. I began to look at people and life through different lenses. I was trying to figure out exactly what God wanted to do with my story. The hurt from the church and my family—my dad, in particular—was difficult to process and heal from. I had to realize that the people who hurt us are human, and their harmful actions are not a reflection of Jesus. Jesus was the one who rescued me from myself and the pit I was in.

The Lord will fulfill his purpose for me; your steadfast love, O Lord, endures forever. Do not forsake the work of your hands (Psalm 138:8 ESV).

As I stepped into adulthood, I had a lot to learn. Even though I had to grow up fast and mature in unexpected ways during high school, there were still things I needed to come to understand and places in my heart that had to grow. The one thing I learned the most was grace.

Grace to forgive.

Grace to see others as Jesus does.

Grace to love people where they are.

Offering grace is only possible through Jesus. I experienced that in my life, and now I've learned to practice this same grace, even to my family. Satan wants to hold us captive to anger, resentment, hurt, and unforgiveness. But God. God works behind the scenes in our hearts to bring forth healing.

God never stopped pursuing me. When I was in college and finding fulfillment in men, He loved me. When I knew what was wrong and still chose sin, He saw me. I have never been unseen by God. I know that His heart was broken, but He chose me. He loved me enough that His loving kindness sought me.

Even as he chose us in him before the foundation of the world, that we should be holy and blameless before him. In love, he predestined us for adoption to himself as sons through Jesus Christ, according to the purpose of his will (Ephesians 1: 4-5 ESV).

I stand in amazement that the God of the universe never left me. I was the lost sheep emotionally in so many ways, and God left the ninety-nine to bring me back to Him. The hurt I had was so deep; yet the inability to understand His plan at the time led me to open my heart and surrender to His complete control. I had a choice. I could harbor feelings of unforgiveness, or I could release those feelings, forgive, and find freedom. God sees the end from the beginning and has a plan when our eyes cannot see it.

> *If a man has a hundred sheep and one of them wanders away, what will he do? Won't he leave the ninety-nine others on the hills and go out to search for the one that is lost? And if he finds it, I tell you the truth, he will rejoice over it more than over the ninety-nine that didn't wander away! In the same way, it is not my heavenly Father's will that even one of these little ones should perish* (Matthew 18:12-14 NLT).

So many times, I have felt like the one lost sheep; sometimes, I still do. God often reminds me that He rejoices over me with singing. He delights in me no matter how broken I am. How can the King of kings delight in me? He takes great pleasure in me because He created me. God knew that my world would be turned upside down in high school, and He prepared me even when I didn't know He was.

The times when I didn't feel seen and heard as I was growing up, God was listening. The times when I needed my earthly father to show up in my life, Jesus was there, being the perfect Father I needed. When my heart was broken into pieces, God placed those pieces together to make an even more beautiful piece of art. God is the potter of our lives. He molds us if we allow him to. God has this way of bringing such beauty from the ashes of our lives. Whatever we walk through, God uses to shape us. Our struggles do not define us, but they can have a significant impact on our lives. Now that I have my own children and family, I consistently reflect on my upbringing, and I can honestly say that gratitude is a word that continually enters my mind.

> *In every situation [no matter what the circumstances] be thankful and continually give thanks to God; for this is the will of God for you in Christ Jesus* (1 Thessalonians 5:18 AMP).

When you feel God might not see you or be listening to your heart cries, know He is ever-present, working behind the scenes. He is with you on the valley floor, sitting criss-cross applesauce. God gently takes a seat next to us, waiting for us to release all the hurts and things that hold us captive. God whispers to our heart, *"I will never leave you or forsake you"* (Hebrews 13:5 ESV). What joy that brings to my soul. The deep crevices of my heart rejoice that He will never leave me.

You Are Not Alone When You Feel Left Out

by Mendez Nelson and Lisa Tofano Hathaway

Have you ever felt left out of something? Today, especially with social media constantly in our faces, it is an all-too-common feeling. From others' highlight reels, it can appear that everyone except you is having the time of their life. Not being included is a hard pill to swallow. Even if what we were left out of was not good for us, it still can be challenging to accept. We vacillate between thinking we should never be excluded because of how nice we think we are and feeling we are not good enough ever to be included.

The Bible gives several examples of people who experienced being profoundly left out. In Genesis 37, Joseph was thrown into a pit and sold into slavery by his brothers, who were motivated by jealousy.

> *But his brothers hated Joseph because their father loved him more than the rest of them. They couldn't say a kind word to him* (Genesis 37:4 NLT).

Similarly, when Jesse assembled all of his sons to be considered to be chosen as king, he left David in the fields, tending to the flocks. You can only imagine how David must have felt. His father and brothers did not include him at all. They did not even consider him worthy of standing with them in front of the priest as he announced who among them would be king. It hits deep in our souls when our family leaves us out and does not seem to care about our feelings in any way. But David's story allows us to see that even when man leaves us out, God includes us in His family.

> But the Lord said to Samuel, "Don't judge by his appearance or height, for I have rejected him. The Lord doesn't see things the way you see them. People judge by outward appearance, but the Lord looks at the heart." (1 Samuel 16:7 NLT).

And God promises this in Psalm 27:10—*For my father and my mother have forsaken me, but the Lord will take me in* (ESV).

God even refers to David later in the Scripture as a man after His own heart.

Women in the Bible often felt left out in society. The Bible is filled with stories about this. For example, Leah's younger sister Rachel, who was very beautiful, was being pursued by a man. Leah's dad said she, as the oldest, had to get married first because of the day's custom; however, when she got married, she was not loved by her husband. The Bible quickly lets us know that Leah was loved by God. He does not leave us out. (Leah's story is told in Genesis 29.)

The woman at the well (John 4) had a bad reputation in town, so she snuck to the well around noon when no one would be there. Or so she thought. But God saw her. He knew her and her need for true love. God sent Jesus to the well that day to show her His love and let her know that, in His eyes, she belonged.

Jesus refers to Himself as The Good Shepherd. He is known to leave the 99 to search for the one who has gone astray. Jesus tells us this parable:

"If a man has a hundred sheep, and one of them wanders away, what will he do? Won't he leave the ninety-nine others on the hills and go out to search for the one that is lost? And if he finds it, I tell you the truth, he will rejoice over it more than over the ninety-nine that didn't wander away!" (Matthew 18:12-13 NLT).

Our Savior never abandons us or leaves us out. Jesus Himself intercedes for us. He loves us so much He laid His glory aside, left heaven, and humbly came to earth as a baby. Isaiah 53:3 tells us that because He was despised and rejected by men, He can relate to how we feel.

The holy and living God is our faithful High Priest who always sees us. We never need to feel left out.

· ·

MALEY MOAK

Maley Moak is passionate about the gospel of Christ and always strives to be a light to everyone she encounters. She is a driven individual whose journey embodies dedication and faith.

Maley graduated from Mississippi State University in 2023 with a degree in communication. Her time as a cheerleader at Mississippi State not only showcased her spirit but also instilled in her the value of teamwork and perseverance.

Currently, Maley is pursuing her next academic milestone at Mississippi College School of Law, where she is serving as student body Vice President, learning the complexities of the law.

Alongside her academic pursuits, she is engaged to Hamilton Williams, an officer in the Marine Corps. Maley and Hamilton plan to get married in June of 2025 and begin their life together.

Maley's long-term goals are to be a military spouse to Hamilton and become a practicing attorney who makes a difference in others' lives.

Maley's journey is a testament to her unwavering determination, faith, and love. She has always loved to write and was called by God to participate in this book!

THE FRIEND WHO ALWAYS SEES YOU

by Maley Moak

If you had known me in college, there is no doubt in my mind you would not have considered me unseen. My Instagram? Flawless. Resume? Flawless. Acquaintances? Too many to count. There wasn't a day I walked across the Mississippi State University campus that at least one person didn't stop to say, "Hey, Maley." I was a cheerleader for the university, spending hours upon hours with girls at practice and even more hours cheering on football, volleyball, and basketball players. And I was in a sorority surrounded by many girls just like myself.

But somehow, some way, I could not have been more alone. College was a place where many people knew of me, but very few truly knew me.

I never had what could be considered a friend group during my four years of college. Ever. But there were three girls who meant the world to me—Claire, Emory, and Addison. All three were distinctively different. Three separate girls who were so important to me, but we were never a "group" of friends.

Claire was my teammate and roommate. She was from Alabama. Addison and Emory were best friends. I had the honor of being friends with them individually, but we weren't a group.

But by my senior year, I was separated even from these three. Claire got married and moved away, Emory left the university as she graduated early, and Addison got married and began working a big girl job. Why in the world would my only three real friends graduate early?

Throughout my undergrad years, I felt the most anxious when I prepared to walk through the doors of my sorority house and knew I would see girls sitting together at tables, laughing, talking, and having a great time. I would walk through the lunch area with my tray and hear, "Hey, Maley, how's your day going?" But all too often, I wanted to flip the trays out of girls' hands and shout that I knew they didn't truly care how my day was going.

Those small talk conversations within the walls of my sorority house destroyed me. They were meaningless acts of obligation. Truly so ingenuine. Empty words.

Finally, I would make it through the lunch line, and it would be time to pick a table. One known group would always be at one table, and another known group was at another. The groups were exclusive; I didn't feel welcome in any of them. I felt like the walls were closing in on me as I tried to pick a table with girls I was supposed to call "sisters." I would quickly choose a place to sit and eat my food, then walk away, realizing that I had sat there for 20 minutes without speaking one word because I was simply not involved in the conversation, and no one cared enough to include me. Fine. Whatever. I had known what to expect before I even walked in— loneliness in a place where hundreds of girls knew me BY NAME.

And then there were the date parties. In high school, I saw so many Instagram pictures of girls in college all dressed up for date parties. I used to look forward to the time I would have a friend group to go to a dance, have fun, and take cute pics with. I dreamed of hanging out with a group of friends I loved, then laying down at night and thanking God for an amazing college experience, the best friends ever, and loads of fun—just like so many portrayed on social media. Let me tell you—those scenarios were nowhere near close to my experience.

Some of my least favorite college memories were the nights of date parties. How? Why? Were those nights really so bad? Let me explain. Allow me to walk you through a typical night in my life as a sorority girl going to a date party.

Let's set the scene: say the date party began at 7:00, and the theme was the 80s.

First, I'd spend all week stressing as I looked for the cutest 80s outfit possible.

At 5:30 the day of, I'd start getting ready—putting on 80s makeup, crimping my hair, and putting on my outfit. At around 6:00, when I was finished getting ready, I'd take cute selfies for Snapchat and then start watching posts. Of MY pledge class, MY "friends." The girls who called me by name every single day and were already hanging out together. They would either be eating a meal together before heading to the venue or having drinks at someone's apartment and, of course, taking cute group pictures. And there I was, sitting by myself at my house, trying to muster up the strength to go to the date party.

Then, I'd go to the date party. Alone. All night. And I'd act like I was having fun as I stuffed feelings of loneliness.

The following day, I'd wake up to see my Instagram feed flooded with group pictures of girls dressed for the 80s, having a great time.

My only question each time this happened was, "What am I doing wrong?"

I truly could not come up with an explanation. I couldn't understand what everyone else was doing that I wasn't. How were they able to live such fun and exciting lives?

Thankfully, my little sister decided to attend the same college I did. She didn't get there until my junior year, so I only had two years with her, but I am forever grateful for those two years. I had someone at least to walk through the doors of date parties with.

Unfortunately, my sister's experiences at college mirrored mine in many ways. During her freshman year, her pledge class went to the beach for spring break. I had to watch my sister as she became one of the only ones not included in the group chat. Her roommate went on the trip. Her bid day friends also went. Literally, everyone was talking about going to the beach for spring break, and I had to comfort my sister as she shed tears over not being invited. But I did not do the one thing I told myself I never would. I did not lie to her. I never told her it would surely get better and that they would include her one day. Because the truth was, there was no guarantee of things happening that way.

I made it through four years of college without ever being invited on a spring break beach trip, winter break ski trip, or even to a friend's home-town for the weekend. My sister soon began to ask the same question I did: "What am I doing wrong?"

Senior year progressed—I was almost out of the darkness of pretending I belonged in places I clearly did not. I was accepted into law school in a city where many of my sorority sisters would be moving, either for graduate school, medical school, nursing school, or dental school. So I did what any other sorority girl would do and started asking around, "Hey! I hear you'll be in the Jackson area next year. I am looking for someone to live with. Do

UNSEEN: YOU ARE NOT ALONE

you need a roommate? Or if not, do you know someone who does?"

It never failed—they either already had living plans with their clique, or they simply didn't take 30 seconds of their day to respond to me. As I sat in a place of pure defeat, the enemy crept in to feed me so many lies: *You're unseen, unheard, overlooked, unwanted, lonely, and simply put—not good enough.*

An alumna from my sorority spoke to our chapter to raise awareness of people on our campus who feel lonely and unseen. She gave us numbers from a survey conducted on campus among Greek-life and non-Greek-life students. The overwhelming majority of students said they feel either alone, unseen, or both. AND I DID NOT EVEN PARTICIPATE IN THE SURVEY. I sank in my seat. I felt as if she were talking directly about me. She was describing every single emotion I felt, but saying that I was supposed to be the one to seek out the people who felt that way. All the while, I kept thinking, "But no one is seeking me out." No one even thought twice that Maley Moak could be in those numbers, but boy was I.

What this told me more than anything is that I was not alone. If I, a cheer-leader and popular sorority girl who was in love with Jesus Christ and had my head on straight, felt completely and utterly alone, what about the people who go home by themselves and don't have anyone who calls them by name? What about the people who haven't made a single true friend in college? What about the people who have never had a friend in Jesus? To those students—I'm sorry. I'm sorry that I have so many blessings to count, and perhaps I'm one of the people who made you feel the way I felt for four years. I'm sorry that social media depicts my life on a silver platter to convince you that I have the best life when I don't. And I'm sorry I didn't write this sooner.

One thing I know—the God of the universe knows you and me by name. *I have called you by name; you are mine. When you go through deep waters, I will be with you. When you go through rivers of difficulty, you will not drown. When you walk through the fire of oppression, you will not be burned up; the flames will not consume you. For I am the Lord, your God, the Holy One of Israel, your Savior* (Isaiah 43:1-3 NLT).

And no matter the amount of loneliness you feel, you were not only worth creating, but you were worth dying for. *But God showed his great love for us by sending Christ to die for us while we were still sinners* (Romans 5:8 NLT). Jesus' perfect sacrifice took on my sin and your sin so that we don't have to feel lonely or unworthy. THOSE DEBILITATING EMOTIONS ARE NOT FROM YOUR CREATOR. *Don't be dejected and sad, for the joy of the Lord is your strength!* (Nehemiah 8:10 NLT). Those negative emotions are the product of the deception of the one who hates you, despises you, and wants to kill you. *The thief's purpose is to steal and kill and destroy. My purpose is to give them a rich and satisfying life* (John 10:10 NLT).

But let's be real for a minute—even if all those things are true (and they are!), how do we fix the fact that we still feel unseen and alone? What's the solution?

From the depths of my being and through the experiences God has given me, I know the solution is fixing our eyes, not on ourselves, but on the one thing that matters—Jesus Christ.

The truth is that many girls you see on social media with dozens of friends live a never-ending cycle of trying to fit in. The fix for loneliness isn't finding a group of friends but knowing who you are in Christ, even when you don't have a single friend.

If we're being honest, some girls who have an ideal-looking friend group and the so-called "perfect" life on social media have created a façade to mask their inner loneliness. And sadly, they may not have developed a relationship with the only perfect friend: Jesus Christ. We each have the opportunity to seek that one friend who will never leave us. When we say yes to God, accepting Jesus as our savior, not only do we gain the best friend ever, but we also gain a SOURCE of joy that is never fleeting, never failing, and filled with abundant love and grace.

Despite knowing this in the depths of my soul and becoming reliant on Jesus, I would be lying if I said I now no longer experience hard days.

There are still days I'm jealous and feel lonely and defeated. But I've learned in my four years of living the college life people dream of that this life will fade away. Through it all, the one and only thing that matters is that I am a disciple of Jesus Christ and make other disciples. Sure, for some, college includes finding their bridesmaids and besties for life and blah blah blah, but then what? What is next? Get married? Okay, cool, then what? Have kids? Yep. So now you've had your dream wedding, dream husband, dream house, dream babies. Now what?

The hard reality is that girls who spend their lives looking for friends to post pictures with often miss out on significant, life-giving moments. SO many girls miss what matters most. And I promise from the bottom of my heart that when those girls lay their heads down at night in a never-ending cycle of trying too hard instead of giving it all to Jesus, they experience a loneliness that nothing in the world can quench.

If you have been battling jealousy, friend group fatigue, or the illusion that you are unseen, please STOP TRYING TO BE SEEN. You can REST in the person that God has created YOU to be, knowing that He sees you. And please hear me—I don't think that God's intentions are to leave you in a place with no friends. We need people. We need mentors, leaders, and people we can confide in. And in His perfect timing, He provides us with those people. Even if it is one single person.

And beyond that, when we feel unseen, perhaps God is calling us to START SEEING OTHERS. If that survey was right, I was never alone in my loneliness. And if I can concentrate on supporting someone else, I think that would make God smile.

Throughout this journey of writing, as I've endeavored to share my struggles with you, God has provided. I will soon be starting law school, and the Lord has provided me with a sweet roommate who is attending the same law school I am. She's from my university, actually from my sorority. In my four years of undergrad, I never even met her. This is proof to me that God's timing is truly perfect. I believe I had to go through so much pain and hurt in the process of looking for a roommate so that the Lord could break me to the point of seeking help and seeking Him, which ultimately led me here—writing this.

The promise we must all rest in is the gospel of John: *Greater love has no one than this, than to lay down one's life for his friends* (John 15:13 NKJV). I can count on one friend who loves me that much—Jesus Christ alone. Because He did. He sacrificed His life for me on a cross so that I can live in eternity with Him. That is the greatest love story of all time.

Heavenly Father,

You are seated on the throne. I can talk to you because Jesus made a way. My prayer for myself and for every single hurting girl reading is that we will be children who believe that you WILL provide the friends we need. But Father, instead of relying on friends to fulfill us, give us a heart posture that believes that EVEN IF you don't, we have all we need in you. Thank you for being our friend when no one else is. Thank you, Jesus, for never leaving me, never forsaking me. Thank you, Jesus, for sacrificing your life for a sinner like me. I love you.

Amen.

You Are Not Alone When You Are Following Jesus

by Maley Moak

Embracing the path of following Jesus can sometimes feel like a solitary journey. I've had moments where tears streamed down my face as I pleaded with God, seeking reassurance that the sacrifices were worth it. I believe every Christian reaches a point where they pause and ask themselves, "Is this truly worth it?"

I think this question in the Christian faith makes logical sense. Jesus told us, *"Whoever wants to be my disciple must deny themselves and take up their cross and follow me. For whoever wants to save their life will lose it, but whoever loses their life for me will find it"* (Matthew 16:24-25 NIV). Jesus laid out a demanding requirement for discipleship: denying oneself and taking up the cross. It's a call to surrender everything—our desires, friendships, habits—and follow Him. This radical commitment can naturally prompt us to question if it's truly worth the sacrifice.

The first step in understanding that you're not alone in following Jesus is to know that it IS worth it; to be able to read that verse from Matthew 16 and let it EXCITE YOU that the King of the world invites you to follow Him. When doubts arise, I find comfort in visualizing Jesus on the cross, a poignant reminder of the immense sacrifice He made on my behalf. I recall advice from a wise man to preach the gospel to myself daily, ensuring I never grow indifferent to the weight of the cross.

Yet, even with this understanding, the Christian journey can still feel isolating. In a world consumed by pursuits divergent from Jesus, it's easy to feel like an outlier or question if we're missing out. This feeling always brings me back to the story of Shadrach, Meshach, and Abednego, who stood firm in their faith amidst a culture hostile to their beliefs. These three young men experienced firsthand the challenges of standing firm in their faith. As captives in Babylon under the rule of King Nebuchadnezzar, they encountered pressure to conform to the Babylonian way of life. Despite undergoing training intended to assimilate them into the foreign culture, their unwavering devotion to God prevented them from compromising their beliefs.

One of my favorite moments in their story, found in the book of Daniel, occurs when King Nebuchadnezzar built a golden statue and demanded that all bow down and worship it. Anyone who did not worship the golden image would be thrown into the fire. In the face of this threat, Shadrach, Meshach, and Abednego boldly declared their faith, stating, *"If we are thrown into the blazing furnace, the God we serve is able to deliver us from it, and he will deliver us from Your Majesty's hand. But EVEN IF he does not, we want you to know, Your Majesty, that we will not serve your gods or worship the image of gold you have set up"* (Daniel 3:17-18 NIV, emphasis added). You may know what happened next: the three men were thrown into the fire, but they did not burn up. Rather, there was a fourth man who appeared in the fire with them—the pre-incarnate Jesus.

When we feel alone in following Jesus, we need to have the same "EVEN IF" attitude that Shadrach, Meshach, and Abednego had. We have to get to a place in our faith that says, "God, EVEN IF I am the only one who is following you, the only one pursuing purity, the only one going to church, the only one missing out on things, I WILL NOT SERVE THE THINGS OF THIS WORLD!"

The truth is that Satan wants you to believe you are all alone. But that's not the heart of our God! Paul says that we are the body of Christ, and each of us is part of it. There are many parts, but one body. So even when we feel alone in our journey with Christ, we can know there is a body of believers who love us! My prayer is that you and I can fully know that following Jesus is worth it and also fully understand that we are not alone in this endeavor. But, EVEN IF we were alone, we would still have a heart to lay down everything to follow Jesus.

. . . .

Kendall Fussell

Kendall Fussell is a graduate of Liberty University. She studied Family and Child Development, Psychology, and Biblical Studies. She plans to obtain her Master of Arts in Religion with a focus in Discipleship and Church Ministry.

Kendall has a deep love for Christ and His Church. Her heart is burdened for the lost and the broken. Wherever the Lord leads her, she hopes to share with others the love that Christ has shown her.

Kendall has always loved to journal, which has become an integral part of her walk with Christ. Through good times and bad, Kendall often found herself with her Bible, pen, and journal. As she grew, so did her love for writing. It was through journaling that she grew in both love and intimacy with her Heavenly Father.

This chapter is the first time her writing will be shared with others!

THE GOD WHO SEES ME
by Kendall Fussell

My dad and I always had a sweet relationship.

I'm the baby of the family and have two older sisters. My dad was the youngest of four boys. We were both the peacemakers of our families—with easy-to-please and go-with-the-flow mentalities. When I was little, I remember my dad telling my sisters and me Bible stories before bed. He would act out the story of David and Goliath with his hands, and I would fall asleep thinking about the power and might of our God.

For years, Daddy took my sisters and me to church every Wednesday night and taught my class truths about God in such a child-like way. He was goofy and silly, not afraid to embarrass himself to keep our attention and teach us about the love of Jesus.

He would drive us to elementary school, and we would sing about rejoicing in the day that the Lord had made.

I remember holding his hands as a little girl and being amazed at how big and strong they were.

As I grew up, we grew more distant. Daddy worked a lot, and I became more involved in sports and school. While he wasn't super engaged in my everyday life, he never failed to remind me how proud he was of me and how much he loved me.

Often, I would only see him right before bed and early in the morning. I would grab his hand before going upstairs at night and tell him I loved him; in the morning, while I was still half asleep, I would rest in his arms.

He would tell me things such as "I'm uber proud of you" and "You're my SHE-ro" (hero, but with an added emphasis to make it "she" instead of "he").

My dad was the king of dad jokes. He loved music, movies, and Mountain Dew.

He wasn't perfect by any means, but he always made sure I knew how much he loved me.

May 10th, 2020.

It was a beautiful spring Sunday morning. The birds were chirping, and the sun was shining brightly. It was Mother's Day. The COVID-19 pandemic was in full force. Life had slowed down from a sprint to a stroll in the park. Everyone was home from school and work. It felt like the Lord hit the pause button on the busyness of our American lives—He was teaching us to slow down and look around instead of running full force past all the beauty surrounding us.

I had woken up early to set out the Mother's Day card and snacks I had gotten for my mom. The sun had just risen and was shining peacefully through my bedroom window. The smell of coffee filled the house. I could hear the news on the TV downstairs.

As I came downstairs, my dad was taking his breakfast into the living room. We smiled and said good morning like we always did. Many mornings started just like this. Mornings were often the time my dad and I would spend together. We both would rise early and soak in the peace and beauty before the chaos of the day began.

After setting up the Mother's Day gifts on the kitchen table, I poured my cup of coffee, grabbed my Bible, and made my way outside to the back porch to spend time with the Lord.

The songs of the birds were sweet in my ears. The warmth of the sun kissed my skin.

I left the back door cracked open so our two little dogs could come and go as they pleased.

I opened my Bible up to Psalm 46. *God Is Our Fortress.* I began reading and praying through the words on the pages.

> *God is our refuge and strength,*
> *a very present help in trouble.*
> *Therefore we will not fear though the earth gives way,*
> *though the mountains be moved into the heart of the sea,*
> *though its waters roar and foam,*
> *though the mountains tremble at its swelling. Selah*
> (Psalm 46 1-3 ESV)

I underlined the words: *God is our refuge and strength, a very present help in trouble.*

Little did I know how much these words would mean to me in the coming minutes, months, and years.

As I reflected on these words, I heard my dad call my name from inside. He sounded like he needed something, so I got up and pushed open the back door.

I had no idea that what would take place in the next hour would change my life forever.

I said, "Yes?" as I entered through the door and saw my dad stammering into the kitchen. "Daddy?" I asked, as my heart began to race. "Daddy, are you okay?"

"I don't know what's happening," he said as his eyes began to roll back in his head. He reached out his arm to me. I grabbed it.

"Daddy!" is all I could say.

Gasping for air, he fell to the floor as I held his arm.

I screamed for my mom to come help.

Within seconds, my mom, two sisters, and I were stammering to call 911 and follow their instructions.

My sister and I began performing CPR. Tears flowed from our faces down onto His chest. His face was turning purple. His chest was hard.

Time seemed to freeze as we counted with the EMS responder over the phone.

"1...2...3...4...5..."

We took turns with the chest compressions as we heard sirens drawing near.

EMS responders rushed into our living room and took over. My mom, sisters, and I moved back into the bedroom to get out of the way.

"God, please save him! Please save him! God, please!" I sobbed through tears.

After a few minutes, we moved outside to our front lawn. Fire trucks, ambulances, and police cars filled our neighborhood.

My sisters and I fell to the ground as we cried and prayed. Neighbors gathered around us, holding us and interceding on our behalf.

My mom had stayed inside with my dad.

We sat there in our front yard, not knowing what was happening or what would come next.

Soon, my mom came around the corner of the house sobbing and shaking her head. She looked up at us and mouthed the words, "He's gone."

There were no words I could say. There was nothing I could do. There I sat, completely distraught and confused. All that would come out were sobs of disbelief.

Word traveled fast. Before I knew it, friends' and families' cars pulled in behind all the first responder vehicles. I ran into the arms of those who knew me best. We sobbed together, all in disbelief.

Chaos surrounded me. Nobody knew what to do. Nobody could believe this was actually happening.

They took us around to the side of our house as the hearse maneuvered through all the other cars and into our driveway.

Again, time seemed to freeze as I looked at the car that I knew would carry my dad's body away.

The next hours are all such a blur.

So many people filled our house. Instantly, our fridge was full of food. Family arrived who I hadn't seen in months. Phone calls took place that just didn't even seem real.

I remember one split second when I looked around and was so happy to see so many people I loved together all at once.

And then I remembered why they were all there.

This just can't be real, was all I could think.

The next few days were the most chaotic yet empty days of my life. It all just felt like a bad dream I would soon wake up from. But I never did.

The funeral came and went. I watched as a big blue box was lowered into the ground. As we drove away from the cemetery, I couldn't accept the fact that my dad's body was now six feet underground.

The following weeks were quiet in the house. Slowly, meals stopped coming, and family members visited less often. I couldn't grasp my new reality. I didn't want to. I was numb and still in complete shock. I remember crying myself to sleep, then waking up just to remember everything that had happened, and the tears would resume again.

People kept saying it would get better with time, but I refused to believe them.

One day, probably a month after my dad passed, I was sitting outside on my front porch swing. I couldn't bring myself to sit on the back porch—it was the last place I sat before my world was shattered, and I just wasn't ready to go back there.

I sat in the swing we bought my dad for the previous Christmas. We always talked about how nice a porch swing would be. And it was. It had become my new favorite place at my house. I sat and stared out into the trees and sky. Tears streamed down my face. I wasn't weeping. I didn't have the energy to weep. I simply sat as the sadness and heartbreak flowed out from within.

I was so weak. I was tired. Exhausted from trying to wrap my head around this new reality. Exhausted from all the emotions I was trying to process. I realized that my heart had never truly been broken before. I was now experiencing what heartbreak was, and I didn't know how my shattered heart would ever be healed.

I had never felt more alone. Not only did I feel misunderstood by everyone around me, but I couldn't even understand myself. I was lost and crushed. I felt so unseen.

I had worship music playing on my phone. I was numb to most of the words. But as I sat, a song came on that I had heard before. The melody was sweet, and it brought me peace. I began listening to the words the artists were singing, which spoke of our beautiful Father and His perfect love.

As I listened to the words, I felt myself sink into the swing. I looked up into the sky as I gently swung back and forth.

I had my Bible and journal opened on my lap. I picked up my pen and started writing. I let my true thoughts and emotions freely flow onto the pages of my journal. For the first time, I was truly fragile and vulnerable before the Lord.

"God. Why? I don't understand any of this. I don't understand how you are good right now. I don't understand how you let this happen. God, why did you let my dad die? Why didn't you save him? Why did this have to happen? How am I supposed to move from here? How am I supposed to live without my dad? Is this really my life? Is this really going to be my story? Am I going to have to tell people for the rest of my life that my dad died when I was 16 years old? Why did I have to see it all? Why was I the one who was there? Why was my name the last name he called? Was there something I could've done to help him more than I did? God! Why?"

Tears continued to pour from my eyes, more than I ever thought possible. I wasn't just crying at this point. I was weeping. Sobbing. Crying out to God. Feeling more pain and heartbreak than I ever knew was possible to feel.

As I gasped for air, trying to calm my breathing, I heard the words of the song whisper between my spiraling thoughts. Reminding me of what I knew to be true. God was holding me in His love. He wanted me to breathe.

My Heavenly Father, in His grace and kindness, was drawing me near.

Breathe, my child. I know. Come rest in my arms. Come to me. I am still here. I promise I'm not going anywhere. You can be honest with me. I know you don't understand. I'm sorry. I'm sorry for the heartbreak you're experiencing right now. It breaks my heart, too. Come to me, my daughter. You are safe with me. I've got you. My arms are loving. My love for you is like no other. It's okay, my girl. Just rest with me here. I'm not going anywhere.

I see what you've been through. I see your heart. I see your pain. I see you.

These moments were when I truly began to fall in love with God. I understood the depth of His love for me in a new way. Looking back, I see that this was the beginning of a true love story.

I found myself marveling over passages of scripture such as Psalm 139:

> *O Lord, you have searched me and known me!*
> *You know when I sit down and when I rise up;*
> *you discern my thoughts from afar.*
> *You search out my path and my lying down*
> *and are acquainted with all my ways.*
> *Even before a word is on my tongue,*
> *behold, O Lord, you know it altogether.*
> *You hem me in, behind and before, and lay your hand upon me.*
> *Such knowledge is too wonderful for me; it is high; I cannot attain it.*
> (Psalm 139:1-6 ESV)

Oh, what sweet love I had found. How could it be that verses like these could be true for a broken girl like me?

Sitting in the swing on my front porch, I reflected back to the morning of May 10th. I remembered that I was reading scripture before I heard my dad call my name from inside. I flipped through the pages of my Bible to read the same words I had read that morning. It was Psalm 46.

> *God is our refuge and strength,*
> *a very present help in trouble.*
> *Therefore we will not fear though the earth gives way,*
> *though the mountains be moved into the heart of the sea,*
> *though its waters roar and foam,*
> *though the mountains tremble at its swelling. Selah*
> (Psalm 46:1-3 ESV)

I was wrecked by the kindness of God—that He would choose to speak these words in His perfect timing. I reflected back on His faithfulness.

He was my refuge and strength, and He was present during my time of trouble. I didn't have to fear, even though my life was being completely flipped upside down and chaos surrounded me. He was there, and He saw me. So I didn't have to be afraid.

Throughout the next weeks and months, God took me on a journey—just me and Him. I began to understand the gospel in a whole new way. I began to see Jesus rightly, for who He is. He was not against me. He was for me, and He was with me.

God began teaching me so many deep truths about Himself. I learned that He hates death just as much as I do. That is why He sent His Son to die on the cross and then resurrected Him three days later—so that we may have eternal life through believing in Him.

I read Romans 6:23 in a new light. *For the wages of sin is death, but the free gift of God is eternal life in Christ Jesus our Lord* (ESV).

I began to understand the depths of sin in this world. The reality is we were not meant to live in this world forever. Because of the sin present in this fallen world, we all will experience an earthly death. Our sin leads to death. But if we believe in the saving work of Jesus Christ, as we die on this earth, we are made fully alive with Christ.

I processed that the moment in which I watched my dad die on this earth was the same moment in which he was actually finding true life.

What peace and comfort I find resting in that truth.

While I miss the love felt on this earth from my earthly father, I am forever changed by the power and beauty of the perfect love of my Heavenly Father.

I cling to these verses in 1 John 4:9-10. *In this the love of God was made manifest among us, that God sent his only Son into the world, so that we may live through him. In this is love, not that we have loved God but that he loved us and sent his Son to be the propitiation for our sins* (ESV).

My heart still hurts today.

I miss my dad. I wish he were here. I always will.

But the security and comfort found in my relationship with my Heavenly Father are unlike all others. I know deeply and fully that He holds every part of my heart. He loved me before I loved Him. He loved me while I was in rebellion to Him. He gave up His Son to be the complete payment for my sins so that I may know Him. This is true and perfect love.

He is my Protector, my Comforter, my Security, my One True Love, my Refuge and Strength, and my Perfect Heavenly Father.

He is the only one who will never leave or forsake me. He offers me more love and grace than I could ever deserve.

He knows me deeply. He loves me fully. And He sees me completely.

You Are Not Alone
in Your Grief

by Mendez Nelson and Lisa Tofano Hathaway

Grief can be crippling. Grief is complex. There is no time limit on our grief. Many of us can live our lives for years not realizing we have unprocessed grief. Although we often associate grief with physical death, grief can also be the result of heartbreak, loss, or anything that causes us pain. If you are grieving, God knows how you feel. He has been there before and has walked this journey.

Grief can consume us in so many different ways. We may not know how to process our grief, leading us to suppress our emotions or develop other unhealthy coping mechanisms. Many may become paralyzed or lash out in anger because their hurt is so deep. If you find yourself stuck in grief, there is hope. That hope is Jesus. God experienced the ultimate grief when He sent His Son Jesus to die on the cross for us. Can you imagine how that must have felt to see your only child die on the cross? That, my friends, is grief. But we do find hope amid grief because we know that God is with us every step of the way.

Beloved brothers and sisters, we want you to be quite certain about the truth concerning those who have passed away so that you won't be overwhelmed with grief like many others who have no hope (1 Thessalonians 4:13 TPT).

Jesus experienced grief, crying and getting angry over Lazarus' death. Even though Jesus was perfect, He still had emotions and feelings.

> *When Jesus looked at Mary and saw her weeping at his feet and all her friends who were with her grieving, he shuddered with emotion and was deeply moved with tenderness and compassion. He said to them, "Where did you bury him?" "Lord, come with us, and we'll show you," they replied. Then tears streamed down Jesus' face* (John 11:33-35 TPT).

When we allow God to help us carry our grief, He will bless us as we walk through any painful season. God created four seasons in nature for us to walk through—each looks different and has unique blessings. Similarly, God guides us through our seasons of grief even as He gifts us with a new perspective. Even though you may not understand or even want the "new perspective," when we take one simple step at a time, trusting Him, we can walk confidently, knowing we will reach the other side of grief. God's love is so real and tangible when we open our eyes to see Him. Sometimes, God allows things to happen in our lives so we can see Him more clearly.

> *Even if he [the Lord] causes suffering, he will show compassion according to the abundance of his faithful love* (Lamentations 3:32 CSB).

Grief has seasons. When you ask God to guide you, He will take you through the seasons, allowing you to experience all He has in store for you. If you are grieving and are unable to process where you are or where you are going, decide to let God have complete control over your circumstances and allow Him to begin to heal your heart and turn your mourning into joy.

> *Weeping may stay overnight, but there is joy in the morning* (Psalm 30:5b CSB).

> *I will turn their mourning into joy, give them consolation, and bring happiness out of grief* (Jeremiah 31:13b CSB).

God has a purpose for your life and will make beauty from the ashes no matter what you walk through.

> *To all who mourn in Israel, he will give a crown of beauty for ashes, a joyous blessing instead of mourning, festive praise instead of despair. In their righteousness, they will be like great oaks that the Lord has planted for his own glory* (Isaiah 61:3 NLT).

When you are grieving, allow God to walk with you, and your journey will become one of healing for your heart and restoration for your soul. He sees you in your grief.

. . . .

OLIVIA LEWIS

Born and raised in Brookhaven, Mississippi, Olivia Lewis embodies a spirit of determination and compassion that shines through every aspect of her life. At 22 years old, Olivia is a junior at Mississippi University for Women, pursuing a degree in speech pathology with aspirations of earning a master's degree in the field.

Her dedication to her studies is matched by her commitment to service and leadership. Olivia is an active member of her college's chapter of The National Student Speech Hearing and Language Association, where she holds the roles of junior class representative and public relations chair. Through these positions, she excels academically and contributes significantly to the community by advocating for those in need of speech and hearing assistance. Olivia also cherishes moments with her family and friends, creating cherished memories.

Beyond her academic and extracurricular achievements, Olivia's faith is the foundation of her identity. Having had a relationship with Jesus Christ since the age of 10, her faith deepened and matured during her college years. She believes wholeheartedly that her purpose is to share the love of Jesus Christ with others, and she fervently prays that her life and chapter in this book reflect this mission.

Jesus Never Leaves Us in Despair

by Olivia Lewis

The transition from high school to college is, without a doubt, an intimidating experience. Whether you are graduating and headed to a university or going to a community college close to home, the bottom line is that college is different from high school, and change does not always come as easily as we hoped.

I want to be transparent that I am not writing this from the viewpoint of a college student who has figured it out—who never gets lonely or feels unseen, unheard, or misunderstood. I am writing this because I have been in the pit, and some days I still am. Maybe you are there now or will find yourself there in the future. But let me encourage you: I have learned that no matter how far we fall, Jesus does not leave us in despair. Although I knew this to be true in my heart and my spirit, my flesh still tried to convince me otherwise during this precarious time of life. I want to share with you the sudden devastation that encompassed me, requiring me to depend on the Lord more deeply than ever before.

When I graduated from high school, I went to a community college in my hometown on an athletic scholarship. I was so excited that what I had been working for would finally be a reality. However, what I thought would be the best year of my life quickly turned into the most heartbreaking.

During my freshman year of college, my grandmother and my uncle were both sick with life-threatening illnesses. In the span of a year, I tragically watched two of the most independent people I have ever known go from commanding every room they ever entered to being spoon-fed every meal. My grandmother passed away in November of my freshman year, and my uncle the following February. Adding that to trying to adjust to college academically, athletically, and socially did not make for a very fun freshman year.

I would often sit in a locker room or dorm room surrounded by twenty-plus other girls, feeling like I was completely isolated—overcome with sadness. The first time I felt like this, I decided to go home to air out my feelings with my mom, like I usually do when something is bothering me. I expected that, with her help and guidance, things would be better the following week. But that is not what happened at all.

When I got home, my mom, who is the go-the-extra-mile, I-can-fix-it, I-can-do-it-myself type of woman whom I had rarely ever seen cry, was curled up in her bed with the lights off and covers pulled above her eyes crying in a way that I will never unhear. That continued for weeks.

I no longer felt like I had my mom to talk to. My friends didn't know what to say. And for the first time in my life, I felt alone. Meanwhile, the devil told me I was alone in my grief and that if I didn't just get over it, I would miss out on all the opportunities to have the time of my life like I was "supposed" to in college. I believed him. That was the loneliest I had ever felt in my life.

Thankfully, the Lord taught me more through this season of my life than I am going to be able to tell you just through a chapter in a book, but I do want to share just a few things He taught me.

The first thing I learned is that hard times WILL come.

If they haven't for you yet, I encourage you to buckle up and get ready because they are coming. In John 16:33, Jesus says, *"I have said these things to you that in me you may have peace. In the world, you will have tribulation. But take heart I have overcome the world"* (ESV). As the sin-fallen, self-absorbed human beings that we are, we love the first part of that verse, and we should; however, we cannot ignore the middle. Jesus promised us that hard times would come, but He promised it hand-in-hand with the fact that He has overcome the world. God has overcome loneliness!

The second lesson that the Lord taught me through this season is that living by faith and walking in obedience with the Lord is a lesson usually learned in the valley.

It is easy to have faith when all is well when you are living the college life you have been picturing since your junior year of high school, and everything is going exactly how you wrote it out in your planner. But what about when it doesn't?

In Matthew 7:24-26, Jesus says, *"Everyone then who hears these words of mine and does them will be like a wise man who built his house on the rock. And the rain fell, and the floods came, and the winds blew and beat on that house, but it did not fall, because it had been founded on the rock. And everyone who hears these words of mine and does not do them will be like a foolish man who built his house on the sand"* (ESV).

If you want to know if your house is built on rock or sand, ask yourself a few questions: When things do not go as planned—perhaps you have been in college for what already seems like a year and you can't seem to find your people or you just simply feel overwhelmed or misunderstood—how do you react? Do you walk in faith, trusting that the Lord has gone before you, or do you question His will?

Walking in faith is the hardest, most challenging part for me. I often have to ask myself, Am I walking by faith or questioning His will? Most of the time, when the Lord is teaching me something in the valley, I'm too caught up in my own desires to recognize it, and I wind up seeing it in the rearview. I pray that your valleys are few and far between, but when you come out of them, don't forget to glance in your rearview mirror because I promise you there is a lesson you don't want to miss there. Praise God for rearview mirrors!

Third, God taught me that I should not only hope to receive grace, but I must also be willing to extend grace.

This lesson was the most convicting for me. In 1 Peter 3:8, we are taught, *Finally, all of you, have unity of mind, sympathy, brotherly love, a tender heart, and a humble mind* (ESV). During most of my freshman year, I was not particularly a joy to be around. I was confused, overwhelmed, grieving, lonely, and mad at my circumstances. I was not a good friend. I had a short fuse, was a basket case all the time, and was completely consumed with my own emotions. I expected my friends to give me a little grace because I was having a hard year; however, I was unwilling to offer others the same grace I expected.

Specifically, I wasn't even willing to extend grace to my own mom.

I didn't treat my mom with sympathy or a tender heart or even consider that she lost people too and was adjusting and grieving. In my mind, she was the adult, and I was the kid, and she needed to be ready to listen to me when I was upset, just like she had for the past 18 years. And when it was time for me to do the same for her, I was selfish. It was all about me.

I had forgotten that we are called not just to have friends but to be a friend, and not just to receive grace but to extend grace. Perhaps remembering this can help us be slow to anger when a roommate, teammate, or sorority sister seems to be the worst friend in the world. We never know what others may be dealing with behind closed doors nor how we can bless them by offering grace or sympathy or patience. And who knows? Maybe one day, you will need the same from them.

My season of grief, confusion, and loneliness, which I allowed to lead me to drift from the life the Lord had for me, lasted throughout my freshman year and most of my sophomore year of college. Finally, after graduating from community college, I decided I was done being sad and feeling alone. I became determined to get over it and have the college experience everyone else but me seemed to be having.

I decided to go to Mississippi State University and constructed an even more extensive picture in my head of exactly how my life would look there. I would go through rush to be in a sorority and would immediately meet my friend group. I determined it would be so easy and the most fun I'd ever had.

I went to Mississippi State as a Junior in the fall of 2022 and rushed and pledged to a sorority, just like I had planned to. But gaining immediate friends and having tons of fun did not automatically come with becoming a member of a group of people as I assumed they would.

I bet you are familiar with the image I had in my head about what I dreamed my life would look like. Let me lay it out for you—the girl who goes off to college, is in a sorority, has 500 friends, is in 25 clubs, has the perfect boyfriend, and, on top of it all, is beautiful and carries a 4.0 GPA. Do you know where I got this image from? Instagram. How stupid is that?

The funny thing about Instagram, or any social media, is that it is completely fake, and we all know it. My Instagram profile is a highlight reel of my life, and I bet some, if not all, of your Instagram profiles are too. And that girl who had the "perfect" college experience; her Instagram profile was fake, too. I know this because I met some of those girls during my first year at Mississippi State, and it turns out they put their pants on one leg at a time, just like me and you. They get lonely, they feel unheard, and they have bad days.

Comparison is the thief of joy.

Perhaps you have heard those words. They are so true.

I have struggled for a long time with being content with where I am. I always felt like I needed to be doing more or have more friends or make better grades or fill in the blank, so I could measure up. I shared these feelings with a group of ladies from my home church, and a very wise woman spoke some truth over me that changed how I viewed contentment. She told me that contentment is not human nature; we are not naturally going to be satisfied with every aspect of our lives all of the time. She said, "Contentment is learned. Pray that you will begin to want what you have."

When I find myself struggling with contentment and comparison, I cling to the words of that wise woman and what we read in 1 Timothy 6:6-7, which says, *But godliness with contentment is great gain, for we brought nothing into the world, and we cannot take anything out of the world* (ESV). I hope you will do the same. I also encourage you to seek guidance from wise and godly women in your life. Listen to what they say, write it down, and underline it twice. It is good stuff.

At the beginning of my first semester at Mississippi State, as soon as I realized how significant a change this was going to be from the life I was used to that was full of people I had known since birth, I realized that I was not going to be able to escape feeling lonely on my own, so, I started praying that the Lord would give me community. I will not tell you that His answer was instantaneous, because it wasn't. But the Lord was so faithful, as always. This made me question, *Why do we forget to ask the Lord for what we need?* I had wondered for months why I was struggling to find community, but all that time, I never asked. Ask God for what you need. He hears your prayers.

Just after my second semester at Mississippi State started, I moved in with a new roommate. It was a completely unexpected move spurred on by "interesting" circumstances. (Anyone who has had a less-than-great living experience during college knows exactly what I mean by "interesting" circumstances.) The girl I moved in with was from the same hometown as me, and though our families were friends, we never really were. To be honest, I was intimidated by her.

My new roommate was a cheerleader at Mississippi State; she was cool. And to be straight with you, I am not that cool. But she had heard about my situation and Facetimed me on a Sunday afternoon to come spend the night with her. I never left. She does not know I am writing about her in this book, and she will probably have a stroke when she reads this, but I prayed for godly community, and God gave me Maley Moak! The way she loved the Lord and loved me and was a friend to me when I really needed one changed my college experience and my life.

Community does not have to be 20 people. Our God can move through just one person, and then that person will introduce you to their friends, and you can do the same for them. And before you even have time to realize it, the Lord has provided a community that is for you by design. Be consistent in your prayers. He hears you. And He WILL answer!

This coming fall, I am supposed to be a senior in college. I just changed my major, and because of that, I am transferring schools, and academically, I will be a junior. I personally think one of the craziest concepts of this life is that an 18- to 21-year-old human being is expected to know what they might want to do for the rest of their life. If that is where you are, or really no matter where you are, start praying right now, asking the Lord to show you what He is calling you to do.

I had a career plan and a major for three years that I said maybe two prayers about, and then I realized I should probably consider asking the Savior of the entire world for His input. Once I started praying daily, He revealed His plan to me. It did not take long for me to realize I was headed in the wrong direction.

Don't be like me. Don't wait three years to ask the God of your salvation where He wants you. But even after asking and maybe even getting a rock-solid, undeniable answer from God, know it's okay to think that the future is scary. Anxiety is something I never really gave much thought to until about three months ago when I found myself so anxious about the future that I literally felt sick to my stomach every day. My thoughts were always flooded with, *What if I changed my major to the wrong thing? What if I can't make the grades? What if I don't get into graduate school? What if I do all of this and then hate my job?* Then, I listened to a sermon about prayer.

The pastor broke prayer down into rooms, and one of the rooms was called the bread room. In this room, you are to ask the Lord for DAILY bread. He said to ask God for what you need only for today, and there will be no room in the margin to ask for what you need for tomorrow.

One of my favorite passages of scripture is Matthew 6:30-34. "*But if God so clothes the grass of the field, which today is alive and tomorrow is thrown into the oven, will he not much more clothe you, O you of little faith? Therefore, do not be anxious, saying, 'What shall we eat?' or 'What shall we drink?' or 'What shall we wear?' For the Gentiles seek after all these things, and your heavenly Father knows that you need them all. But seek first the kingdom of God and his righteousness, and all these things will be added to you. Therefore do not be anxious about tomorrow, for tomorrow will be anxious for itself. Sufficient for the day is its own trouble"* (ESV).

How silly of me to get caught up in the next five years. Did I honestly think God would not provide for the creation He made in His very own image? Of course He would! I pray that brings you the peace it brings me.

I have never been this vulnerable in sharing about the struggles I had through college. And it was not easy for me to write them down. But the truth is that through it all, the Lord consistently replaced every lonely, disconnected, unseen, or unheard thought, emotion, and season I had with godly community, wise council, a church that has helped me grow more than I could have ever imagined, and His unfailing love. That is why I am sharing this with you.

We all experience some of these feelings as we step out into this world. When you experience them and feel like you are in the pit, please remember you are not alone. Turn to God as you encounter change, loneliness, or even unexpected turmoil; He will make sure, with His grace and love, that you will NEVER be left alone! He has a plan for you to grow and become all He has called you to be in the community He has designed just for you.

You Are Not Alone in Your Loneliness

by Olivia Lewis

Loneliness. I vividly remember seasons in my life when loneliness scared me to death, and sometimes, it still does.

Loneliness can be defined as being without companions. We all experience moments, maybe even days or weeks, of loneliness. My prayer is the Lord will speak through me, a college student who still sometimes struggles with loneliness, to encourage you to cling to His presence and truth during your times of loneliness. If you find your worth in Jesus Christ, every lonely moment you encounter will pale in comparison to the eternity we get to look forward to as children of God.

But let's be real. When you're sitting alone, and every so-called "friend" you thought you had is out doing this or that on a Friday night, and you didn't get the invite, your first thought will not be, *Well, that's fine. I just won't feel lonely because I know, in comparison to eternity with Jesus, the next eight hours of seeing Snapchat stories and Instagram posts of everyone I know having the time of their life is nothing.* That is not human nature. And that's not reality. And, to be blunt, sometimes those nights of sitting alone while all your friends seem to be living the dream will feel a lot longer than just eight hours. And that is okay.

In my own life, I believe that the Lord grew my relationship with Him most in my seasons of loneliness. However, it took me longer than I would like to admit to recognize that I was never truly alone. So please hear me when I say—but most importantly, believe it when you read it from the Creator Himself—neither are you.

> *Trust in him at all times, you people; pour your hearts out to him, for God is our refuge* (Psalm 62:8 NIV).

The word refuge literally means shelter. So, in this verse, our Father is telling us that He is our shelter. Our shelter from loneliness. Our shelter from exclusion. What a comfort it is to know that we can find shelter from every hard day in the hand of the God of our salvation!

If you are anything like me, or honestly, most of us, the devil will attack you during your seasons of loneliness. He will fill your mind with thoughts like, *Just be friends with them even if they're not pursuing the Lord because, if you don't, you won't have any friends. ... Just go out and party like everyone else; it's not that big of a deal. ... If you like the boy, just go out with him. It does not matter what kind of life he lives. It will not affect you.* I could go on for hours, but you get the picture.

When the devil attacks you with these thoughts, stand firm on your convictions and in your relationship with Jesus Christ and run to Him in prayer. Pray that He will give you a community that is seeking Him. Pray that you will be fulfilled by Him alone.

There will always be people who seem like their life is a movie—people who go out every night and have what appears to be the most fun imaginable at parties that seem as if all the A-list celebrities are at. And there will be boys. Lots of boys who seem like "good guys" who just need to grow into their potential. Don't date potential! Date proven character! Flee from every single one of these things. In the long run, they will leave you empty every time.

It is easy to settle in seasons of loneliness, but we are not called to settle. We are called to live a life that is set apart from the world. Sometimes, that might leave us feeling lonely for a moment, but the Lord hears you when you call out to Him. And if you consistently pray and seek community that will lead, love, and guide you, the Lord will remain faithful in providing that for you in His time.

Lean into His presence, His consistency, and His faithfulness. It's worth the wait. You are not alone in your loneliness.

. . . .

CAITLYN BENEDIK

Caitlyn Benedik is a faithful follower of Christ. She is passionate about serving and loving, as Jesus does, whomever she comes into contact with.

As a believer, Caitlyn has been able to serve the Lord in many ways, including growing her high school FCA, going on mission trips to Ecuador, serving at a transitional housing ministry, and being on the leadership team for youth ministries at her church.

Being an athlete all her life, the Lord has guided Caitlyn to a ministry in athletics. Having held many positions in the sports world, she currently serves as a Strength and Conditioning Coach for Division 1 athletes. Caitlyn strives to be set apart and a light for Jesus in a world where fame and fortune are the focus.

Alongside coaching, Caitlyn loves to play pickleball, attend church, and spend time outside and with her family. She also loves to participate in Bible studies and surround herself with Godly community as she firmly believes that when two or more are gathered, the Lord is present.

Caitlyn has felt called to share her story; writing this chapter is a step of obedience!

Beauty in the Broken

by Caitlyn Benedik

The word that came to Jeremiah from the Lord: "Arise, and
go down to the potter's house, and there I will let you hear
my words." So I went down to the potter's house, and there
he was working at his wheel. And the vessel he was making
of clay was spoiled in the potter's hand, and he reworked it
into another vessel, as it seemed good to the potter to do.

Then the word of the Lord came to me: "O house of Israel,
can I not do with you as this potter has done? declares the
Lord. Behold, like the clay in the potter's hand, so are you in
my hand, O house of Israel. If at any time I declare concerning
a nation or a kingdom, that I will pluck up and break down
and destroy it, and if that nation, concerning which I have
spoken, turns from its evil, I will relent of the disaster that I
intended to do to it. And if at any time I declare concerning
a nation or a kingdom that I will build and plant it, and
if it does evil in my sight, not listening to my voice, then I
will relent of the good that I had intended to do to it."
Jeremiah 18:1-10 (ESV)

Art is captivating. It evokes intense emotions that are a reflection of the
piece's creator. Art allows the viewer to see, feel, and understand so much

about the artist.

Mr. Porter wanted to be an artist for this reason. He chose, more specifically, to be a potter. He loved the feeling of the clay running through his hands. But what he truly cherished was how, even when an unskilled observer could see no direction in the lump of clay before him, he had a plan to form something beautiful out of what appeared to be a muddy mess.

It was a crisp fall morning. The sun burst through the clouds, and the birds were wide awake, singing and dancing. Like every other morning, Mr. Porter was at his wheel. He was working on a pot, the featured piece for an upcoming art show that would be auctioned for charity. Deep into his work, Mr. Porter was lost within himself as he manipulated the clay when his neighbor Jeremy entered un-noticeably to watch quietly. Catching a shadow out of the corner of his eye, Mr. Porter's' head and hands jerked up, startled. The artisan looked down at his now-ruined pot—with a gash from the sculpting tool and an entire piece inadvertently torn off. Discouraged but not defeated, Mr. Porter, instead of trashing his clay and getting new, reshaped his disfigured pot back to a ball of clay and reformed it into an even better piece of pottery. Finally, after a long day of shaping and molding, the pot was finished. Leaving it on the rack to dry and set, Mr. Porter, with his hands tired and achy, called it a night.

The next morning, Mr. Porter had renewed energy from a restful night of sleep. Excitement was in the air as he was ready to add color to his creation to make it come alive. Painting for him was about the story inside of him. He always drew from his experiences, whether it was the challenges he faced, the accomplishments he gloried in, or the simple things that made life all worthwhile. He always wanted to leave a little bit of himself in everything he created, which allowed each piece to become his masterpiece. After the pot was painted, Mr. Porter walked over and set it in the kiln—the firing would take the pot from dull to radiant and clear. The firing process was lengthy, and while he was waiting, Mr. Porter's stomach started to growl as if on cue, letting him know it was time for lunch.

As was his daily routine, Mr. Porter grabbed his keys, fired up the engine, and headed down to his favorite place, Heaven's Diner. He loved going there and watching his community grow up in front of his eyes. As soon as he stepped into the door of the diner, he was always greeted with hugs from the little ones. Throughout his lunch, people of all ages, spaces, and places would visit with him—a pillar of love and wisdom in his community. Mr. Porter enjoyed imparting knowledge and truth to those around him. His passion was to help others establish guardrails for their lives so they could resist temptation, flee from evil, and live long and prosperous lives. He always left the diner filled with joy, having seen all those he had been able to help along the way and praying they were heading out to the world to do the same.

Hours later, with a happy stomach and a full heart, Mr. Porter returned home. Knowing he couldn't remove his pot from the kiln until the next day, he walked over to Jeremy's house to see why he had dropped in the day before. Jeremy had a rather large family, and Mr. Porter came to find out that there was a lot of strife with his children. They were not obedient to the rules of his house and openly disregarded his authority. Jeremy was struggling with what to do as he didn't want to lose his children and knew a precedence needed to be set. After hearing what Jeremy had to say, Mr. Porter responded with a simple question, "When you were watching me yesterday, what did you take away?" After thinking a minute, Jeremy knew what to do. After being thanked for his time, Mr. Porter left and returned home.

It was Wednesday, and the pot was finally ready to be removed from the kiln. Mr. Porter was elated with how this piece had turned out and knew it was perfect for tying in his whole display. As he took the pot out and began to walk towards his shelf, he slipped on a rock and stumbled forward. The next thing he knew, the pot flew out of his hands, causing a loud crash as it shattered. Sitting on the ground, deflated and almost in tears, Mr. Porter began to pick up the pieces one by one. He had no idea what he would do as the art show was in two days, and there wasn't enough time to recreate his centerpiece. Unsure of how to proceed, Mr. Porter decided to call it a night and re-approach the situation in the morning.

The next day, Mr. Porter walked into his studio and peered into the box of broken pieces. He took a deep breath to clear his mind and suddenly remembered one word, "Kintsugi." Kintsugi is a Japanese word that means golden joinery. This is a Japanese art where broken pottery is repaired with lacquer mixed with gold. Shrugging his shoulders and thinking to himself, "What do I have to lose?" Mr. Porter decided to give it a shot. So, he spent the rest of the afternoon mending the pot back together, and as the pot began to retake its original shape, Mr. Porter began to regain hope that his creation would be complete.

It was finally time to put his work on display, and Mr. Porter, spilling with anticipation, loaded up his red pickup truck with his pottery and made his way downtown to the gallery. He was a bit on edge as he set up, not knowing how his art would be accepted. He had never displayed anything short of perfection, and his centerpiece was full of cracks. He only wanted to help raise money for the local charity, but now he felt inadequate as his pot was just short of a failure. With his nerves running high, Mr. Porter stepped outside to clear his mind and get some fresh air. He had done everything he could to create the best pottery possible, and now he had to trust that the people would find beauty in the rest of his work.

Not too long after Mr. Porter stepped outside, the host came to inform him that the auction had begun. Leaning against the wall in the back of the room, he watched as the other pieces of art were sold. It was now time for his collection. As the auctioneer began, the bidding number quickly started to rise. Soon, Mr. Porter perked up, surprised at what he heard. He never believed that this broken pot would ever be worth what was being bid, but lo and behold, his pot sold for more than he had ever sold any of his work during his time as a potter.

As the room cleared, Mr. Porter was still standing in shock. On his way out, he decided to find the buyer. Stopping the buyer, Mr. Porter introduced himself and asked him the simple question, "Why?"

The buyer's name was Christian, and he replied, "Mr. Porter, your pot really spoke to me. All my life, I felt broken, not valued, and like my life held no meaning. As I began to grow, my mindset shifted, and instead of allowing my brokenness to define me, I let the cracks become the place where the light could shine that much brighter. It was my brokenness that made me unique and valuable. As I began to embrace that, I found that my story was able to heal and mend others the way it had me. This is why I bought your piece for the price I did. Its brokenness made it priceless, and I was willing to spend as much as I needed to because the journey of making that creation whole was where the beauty began for me. To see that pot shining in the light, broken yet whole, gave it value far beyond what I paid for it."

Speechless, Mr. Porter thanked Chrisitan for his time, hopped in his car filled with gratitude and a new perspective, and drove home.

My name is Caitlyn. The broken yet whole pot in this fictional story resembles my life.

I was brought into this world whole, full of life, determination, and the readiness to grow into a beautiful young lady. Not too long after I was born, the trials of life began. When I was a year old, my parents decided to part ways and end their marriage. Both parents remarried, and neither home was a place I felt safe or loved. In my life, they were supposed to be the potters who would shape me with care and love to help turn me into a secure woman who had the confidence to face anything that came her way. Unfortunately, this is not how my life played out.

My parents' words were sharp, their rage was frightening, and the result was that my home felt like a place to escape from instead of a place to run to. I was marred and scarred, and as I began to face the fire of life, those around who were transporting me out of the fire slipped and dropped me, leaving me shattered. All my life, I was mishandled by those I should have been able to trust to carry me with care and caution. As I got older, I began to believe the lies of inadequacy. I felt as if I would never measure up and could never be loved for who I was, which created an unhealthy desire to reach perfection, hardening my heart. I desired community, but I kept myself closed off. I longed for belonging and purpose but always thought my life held no value. The lies about me I had heard my whole life became my identity, and anxiety slowly started to creep its way in.

Life outside of my home was just as intense. I was an athlete in sports that demanded perfection. I grew up doing gymnastics until tenth grade, and then I switched to playing basketball. Every move of a gymnast is scrutinized and judged. For 12 years, I was criticized and picked apart for every little mistake.

Through my home and sports, I learned early on that if I could manage to do nothing wrong, I would be able to move through life unseen and unnoticed. Therefore, perfection became a coping mechanism for me to hide from the abuse. I became extremely insecure. Between home and gymnastics, I felt like I was always getting hit with the one-two knockout combo; no matter where I turned, I was always being told what I was—

weak, too tomboyish, selfish, lazy, not good enough, or a crybaby. These words became planted in my mind, and I silently began to fight against them. I tried to prove my worth to people, and for the longest time, I thought this was the right way to overcome all the negativity. My life became about chasing success. I believed if I could hoist a trophy, my value would be proven through cemented success that nobody could ever take away from me.

In high school, success was graduating with as many college credits as possible and earning a chance to play college basketball. In college, it was trying to graduate early and win a national championship. When I began to coach high school basketball, success was winning a state championship. Then, to put the cherry on top, I went on to coach men's college basketball to prove to the whole world I could do what only a small fraction of women had been able to do, and not only would I do it, but I was going to be the best at it.

Every day, for as long as I can remember, I lived life with this chip on my shoulder, desiring affirmation and belonging, and that whole time, I was looking in all the wrong places. My drive separated me from my friends and teammates. I was liked by everyone, but I always felt like I belonged nowhere. My name was very recognizable, but I never truly felt known. If I could have stood in a sea of everyone I knew, life would go on around me, but I would be left unseen, unknown, and invisible to the world. My life existed in pieces that felt as sharp and misshapen as broken pottery.

For so long, I lived my life alone. It was me and only me, and I became extremely independent. My drive buried me, and my desire isolated me. Running from my pain, I unknowingly used my work as an excuse to avoid opening myself up to people. I kept those around me at an arm's distance because I had a long history of being abandoned and hurt, and I never wanted to feel that pain again. So, instead, I chose the pain of isolation and loneliness. This tradeoff was neither fulfilling nor anything close to what I needed. Luckily for me, I had a long-time friend named Jesus.

All my life, I have known and loved God. It has always seemed that I was born to follow Him. In the midst of all the chaos, He was my guiding light. I clung to Him and to my faith because He was the one place I could find consistency. He held me together.

No matter what happened, I always had God by my side. He would hold me when I was broken. He would walk with me when I was alone. He would celebrate with me when I achieved something. He would protect me when I started to stray. God was always there to be and provide what I needed. He never failed me or abandoned me; He always ran hard after me. So, as I continued to walk this journey separated from the world, I drew closer to the presence of God.

When I went to undergrad, I was running from everything I left behind at home. It so happened that I went to play basketball at a Christian college, and though I didn't know it at the time, going to a Christian school was probably one of the best choices I could have ever made. For four years, I was surrounded by and held accountable to know God's Word. Though this time was extremely challenging, it helped me begin to define the boundaries of my life. I was still traveling this road alone, but God was with me every step of the way. I learned how to lean into Him and be fully immersed in His presence.

After graduating and taking a year off, I went back to school to get my master's degree, where the ground I had been tilling for years finally started to bloom. I found a church home that embraced who I was and loved me right where they found me. I was blessed with a group of friends who saw me for who God created me to be instead of how I defined myself, which was by my pain. And I was finally in a place where I could stop running and face my pain and my fears. My heart was pieced back together, and my story was no longer one of shame but victory. My cracks and brokenness were mended by the glory of God, and He began using my scars to make me more valuable than I would have been had I never faced the storms of life.

Now, as I sit here, I can truly say that I am fearfully and wonderfully made (Psalm 139:14). I am God's masterpiece (Ephesians 2:10). I am whole, created for a purpose, and needed in the kingdom of God. I can stand tall with my head held high as I walk in courage and boldness as a daughter of the one true King.

Though this journey that I continue to walk still gets lonely at times, there is one thing I have learned. God will never leave me nor forsake me (Hebrews 13:5), and as He walks with me through the fire, He will be a lamp unto my feet and a light unto my path (Psalm 119:105). Though this light may never show me the whole path, I will always know where my next step needs to be.

God is our Potter—our Master Craftsman. You are His masterpiece. From the beginning of time, He had a plan for you, His creation. When you allow His hands to form and shape you, you can be assured that others will see His magnificent artistry and understand Him on an even deeper level through His artistry in you. So even when your life feels broken, know that God is at work—He isn't finished with you. And He is bigger than your brokenness. All we each have to do is continually give God the pieces of our lives and watch as He molds us into a masterpiece worth far more than we can imagine—one that reflects His glory for eternity.

You Are Not Alone in Unexpected Storms

by Mendez Nelson

Again and again in the Bible, we see the devil send storms targeting God's people. So we shouldn't be surprised when we face unexpected storms. But God always brings deliverance in His perfect timing to His children. As we walk through life, we can learn to recognize the devil's schemes and, when we come up against them, fight with the armor God has provided for us as we lean on Jesus, knowing He will always be our deliverer.

Attacks and storms are not just in our minds; they are real. In Ephesians, Paul recognizes this. *For our struggle is not against flesh and blood, but against the rulers, against the authorities, against the powers of this dark world and against the spiritual forces of evil in the heavenly realms* (Ephesians 6:12 NIV).

Unseen forces are present in our daily lives. These entities are responsible for putting thoughts into our minds that are not from God or us. Their goal is to keep us away from God and His purpose for our lives. We must always be on guard against the lies of the devil. One of his tricks is to invite us to believe that we are the big one and God is the small one—that we are more important than God. As a result, we might try to be in control over God. Sadly, we can even begin to think that God was made for us instead of the reality that He created us from His love. Our pride and ego, egged on by whisperings from the devil, can cause us to get things backward and walk directly into the path of a storm.

But God has given us His armor to protect us. Among other things, He teaches us to buckle His belt of truth around our waist because He knows we get hit with so many lies. Picture a boxer preparing to enter the ring to fight. He must be prepared, equipped, and trained. So should we. As the enemy bombards us with assaults on our lives, God reminds us of the armor He gives us.

> *Therefore put on the full armor of God, so that when the day of evil comes, you may be able to stand your ground, and after you have done everything, to stand. Stand firm then, with the belt of truth buckled around your waist, with the breastplate of righteousness in place, and with your feet fitted with the readiness that comes from the gospel of peace. In addition to all this, take up the shield of faith, with which you can extinguish all the flaming arrows of the evil one. Take the helmet of salvation and the sword of the Spirit, which is the word of God. And pray in the Spirit on all occasions with all kinds of prayers and requests. With this in mind, be alert and always keep on praying for all the Lord's people.* (Ephesians 6:13-18 NIV).

Not only do we have the weapons God has given us, but Jesus Himself is always with us in our storms and battles. Jesus promised us, *"And surely I am with you always, to the very end of the age."* (Matthew 28:20b NIV).

In Mark 4:37-39, we see evidence of God's deliverance from a literal storm when Jesus is in a boat with his disciples. *A furious squall came up, and the waves broke over the boat, so that it was nearly swamped. Jesus was in the stern, sleeping on a cushion. The disciples woke him and said to him, "Teacher, don't you care if we drown?" He got up, rebuked the wind and said to the waves, "Quiet! Be still!" then the wind died down and it was completely calm* (NIV).

The devil is no match for God.

Still, sudden storms can be overwhelming and frightening. But we never have to handle them alone. We should not wait until a crisis hits to build a foundation and relationship with God. Because with God as our solid rock and foundation, we will be prepared for the unexpected.

Jesus explained it like this, *"Therefore everyone who hears these words of mine and puts them into practice is like a wise man who built his house of the rock. The rain came down, the streams rose, and the winds blew and against that house; yet it did not fall, because it had its foundation on the rock. But everyone who hears these words of mine and does not put them into practice is like a foolish man who built his house on sand. The rain came down, the streams rose, and the winds blew and beat against that house, and it fell with a great crash."* (Matthew 7: 24-27 NIV).

Although the devil can bring storms against us, he cannot defeat our God.

When God is for us, no one can successfully be against us. Even when weapons are formed against us, they will not prosper. Storms can be devastating and destructive, but God is always on our side, no matter what may come against us. Some storms leave us with broken hearts, while others may cause us to feel hopeless and like we can't go on living. But Jesus will always stand by us as our hope and healer.

Jesus quoted the prophet Isaiah, attributing the words to Himself: *"The Spirit of the Sovereign Lord is on me, because the Lord has anointed me to proclaim good news to the poor. He has sent me to bind up the brokenhearted, to proclaim freedom for the captives and release from darkness for the prisoners."* (Luke 4:18 NIV). Hallelujah! This is good news for us, especially considering all the storms we may still have to face.

No matter how hard any unexpected storm hits you, armor up and trust God's presence and provision. You are never alone in a storm.

. . . .

KATIE WHITEHEAD

Katie Whitehead loves the Lord and sharing His love with others.

She is from Roxie, Mississippi, and is currently a student at the University of Southern Mississippi.

Katie enjoys singing and worshiping the Lord. She serves on the worship team at the Southern Miss BSU. Katie is an artist who loves to glorify the Lord through drawing, painting, and sharing her art with everyone she meets. She also loves spending her summers serving the Lord as a cabin leader at Camp Garaywa, where she has the opportunity to teach God's Word and share the love of Christ with girls in 4th through the 6th grade.

Katie's favorite Bible verse is 2 Corinthians 5:17 (NLT): *This means that anyone who belongs to Christ has become a new person. The old life is gone; a new life has begun!*

She loves to collect and paint butterflies because it reminds her of the hope we have in Jesus and the new life we have in Christ!

UNINVITED, YET INVITED

by Katie Whitehead

Take a moment and imagine this: You walk into an empty room and feel a sudden wave of foreboding emotions. This feeling is not unusual; in fact, it seems familiar. You have felt it before.

Have you ever experienced something like this? I have.

For me, this sudden wave of emotion is a heavy, hurtful feeling that occurs in my chest and sometimes takes over my whole body—extending to my wrists and even down to the bottoms of my feet. The overwhelming feeling takes my breath away and leaves me with tears streaming down my face and words and thoughts spinning in my head. It hurts so much that it feels never-ending. I wish I could just disappear so it would all go away. At the same time, I longed for someone to come rescue me from the pain and tell me it will all be okay.

But I am all alone as the thoughts continue to spin: *No one likes me. Why would they like me anyway? There is something wrong with me. I will never be like other people.*

I have been plagued with thoughts and feelings like this for as long as I can remember. *I do not like to be alone. I need to be around people. I just want all of this to end.*

Struggling with uncontrollable emotions is challenging. I don't want to feel all these things, but for some reason I do. I try to stop the racing thoughts going through my mind, but all my attempts are unsuccessful. The anxiety even causes me to pick the skin around my fingernails for relief. I don't want to isolate myself from others but to feel calm when I am with them. I long to erase the ever-present worries about what others might think about me and the degrading thoughts I have of myself. I am not the person I want to be. I am not the person I believe God wants me to be. I am all alone in my feelings.

I just want to be free.

I have always loved to have one-on-one time with people, even if it is just sitting in the same room with that person in silence—studying, talking, or listening to music. I tend to keep my circle small. In my sophomore year of college, I had a roommate I did everything with. We would wake up in the mornings, read our Bibles together, go out to eat, and just talk and study. I loved that we were roommates and got along so well.

But all of a sudden, everything changed. My roommate became friends with the girls who lived right across the hall from us and stopped hanging out with me. I would ask if we could do something together, and she would say she had other plans. *Why doesn't she like me anymore?* I thought. I began to think about who I was and consider that maybe we were not as similar as I thought. I tried to join in and hang out with her and her friends, but they didn't seem to like me too much. I felt left out, which was more painful than I can explain.

I wasn't invited to do things with them, and my roommate was never in our room anymore. She was always gone, and even when she was there, she didn't seem interested in talking to me. That left me feeling overwhelmingly lonely and as if I wasn't good enough. *Do I need to change? What is it about me? If she doesn't like me anymore, will other people like me?* It got to the point where every time I walked into that room, I felt alone and sad. She even moved her bed out of our room. I knew she wasn't coming back. I was all alone with no one to study with me at night or to sit and listen to music with and read our Bibles like we always used to do.

I struggled with depression and anxiety. I still do some days, but now I have learned to lean on Jesus because He is my hope. Many nights, I would lay in bed and cry myself to sleep. I was experiencing a lot of grief from the loss of family members mixed with emotions of self-hatred. My mind was constantly restless. *I have no purpose because I make so many mistakes,* I thought. *I am such a failure. I am not good enough.* I felt God was disappointed in me. Sometimes, I even considered that my life wasn't worth living. These thoughts would dominate my mind. It seemed never-ending.

I was very quiet about my struggle. I didn't talk to many people about my feelings besides a few close friends. When I did, my friends would tell me to look to God's Word for truth, turn to Jesus, and speak truth over the lies of the enemy. For a while, I didn't listen to them as I was overcome by negative emotions I thought would never end. Eventually, I tried to listen to them and take their advice, but there was so much inside me saying, *No, it won't help. You are stuck here.*

I had often walked around all day, acting like nothing was happening, with an overwhelming hurt in my chest. I had so many emotions of fear, sadness, and anger that I would allow to envelop me. I listened to all the evil thoughts in my head and believed all the lies—until I realized that I was believing lies about myself and became absolutely sick of all of it. So, I finally listened to my friends and started to turn to Jesus and combat the lies with God's truth. It was not easy, but God brought me through, and He continues to fight against the enemy for me with the truth of His Word every day in my life.

After my roommate started to ignore me, it seemed as if I was wrestling with all those lies and feelings all over again because I felt so alone. Being alone brought so many thoughts back to my mind about myself that I did not like. It was exhausting. I remember just wishing that all the pain would end.

The most important part about my story is I didn't let the emotions defeat me even though it felt like they would. I didn't allow the dark thoughts and bad feelings to overcome me. This internal battle was extremely difficult. I wondered why I was going through all these overwhelming feelings again, but I still forced myself to look to the scriptures the best I could. I would sit on my dorm room bed for hours and pray through tears, asking God to take this away from me and help me. I hated the feelings I had about what I was going through, and I held onto Jesus and reminded myself that He was with me because He was right there in that room with me always, and He understood what I was going through.

I knew that the lies and my feelings were not the truth. I learned to stand in front of the mirror, look at myself, and speak the truths of God out loud, which helped me believe the truth instead of the lies. Jesus had brought me through before, and He would continue to help me through this struggle. I cried out for His help in the middle of my sorrow and feelings of loneliness. In a way, my whole world felt dark, But Christ is and was my light. *The light of Jesus can always overcome the darkness. John 1:5 says, The light shines in the darkness and the darkness will not overcome it* (NIV). The wrong thoughts I was thinking about myself—how I was not like others, needed to change, was not good enough, and no one liked me—were all lies from the enemy.

It has taken me a while to learn this. I am still learning.

The only way to combat and defeat the lies of the enemy is with the truth of God's Word. When you find yourself lost in the sea of the enemy's lies, keep searching for God's truth until you find Him.

The lie I believed was that I was not like everyone else and, therefore, I was not good enough. When I replaced that lie with God's truth that says I am unique, created with purpose, and beautifully made by God, my whole perspective of myself changed. Ephesians 2:10 says, *For we are God's masterpiece. He has created us anew in Christ Jesus, so we can do things he planned for us long ago* (NLT). As an artist, I love this verse because it's saying I am God's cherished artwork. A masterpiece isn't just thrown together. Every single detail in the picture is planned and created for a purpose. God created me with purpose; He thought out everything—how He would create my life and everything I would do during my life. And He created you to be unique and beautiful in your own way for a purpose, too.

God showed me that He was listening. He answered my prayers by showing me how much He loves me in a way I did not expect. One night, I was in my dorm room. It was a typical night for me—I was by myself, reading my Bible and praying for God to help me, when I heard a knock on my door. It was late. I was already tired. My eyes were probably still red and heavy from crying while I was praying. I was just about to go to bed and almost ignored the knock at the door. *It must be someone looking for my roommate,* I thought to myself.

Despite my feelings about getting up, opening the door, and possibly getting upset, I forced myself to open the door anyway. Standing right there before my eyes was a sweet girl who played in the college marching band with me. She had hurt her ankle badly while skateboarding and did not have her phone. She was extremely upset and in a lot of pain, so I tried my best to comfort her. I let her use my phone, took care of her, and gave her a snack and some ice for her ankle to help relieve some of the pain. I also asked if I could pray for her, and we prayed together. It was a special moment which she appreciated.

God led her to knock on my door late at night because He knew she could count on me to help her in her time of need. He knew I was a loving and caring person, and I would do anything for her at any time. He was showing me this truth and showing her as well. God used her to show me that night that I do have a purpose and I am loved. He showed me He created me to love people, and I am unique in my own way. He created me to use the spiritual gifts He has given me for His purposes.

The Lord is always near to you. Philippians 4:6-7 instructs us, *Don't worry about anything; instead, pray about everything. Tell God what you need and thank him for all he has done. Then you will experience God's peace, which exceeds anything we can understand. His peace will guard your hearts and minds as you live in Christ Jesus* (NLT).

When I was struggling with my feelings, I would just talk to Jesus and tell Him how I was feeling, and He would give me peace—confirming He was with me, right beside me. Sometimes, it would help me to picture Jesus standing or sitting beside me in the room; He was there with me while I spoke and cried out to Him. *Those who look to him for help will be radiant with joy; no shadow of shame will darken their faces* (Psalm 34:5 NLT). *The Lord is close to the brokenhearted; he rescues those whose spirits are crushed* (Psalm 34:18 NIV).

God kept moving and working in my life. He led me to work at a camp that summer. I was so excited to make new friends and put into practice what God was teaching me. I loved it there, and I loved all the people I worked with. But one day, I watched as everyone made plans to go out to eat and celebrate another great week at camp. No one invited me to go. It really hurt my feelings that I was left out. *Am I invisible? We spent all week together. Why wasn't I invited?* This was devastating. I couldn't believe this was happening to me again, but I quickly looked to the Lord and talked to Him about how I was feeling. He reminded me of how awesome that week had been, that He was always with me, and that it was okay not to be invited. Then He told me He wanted me to spend time with Him and celebrate the week with Him in joy.

Although I was not invited to many things with my friends and roommate, I was invited to do something even greater—to spend time in the presence of my Savior.

Even when life gets difficult, and we are disappointed and let down, God invites us to spend time with Him. He is always there when we need Him, and He wants us to spend time with Him. It sure is a beautiful thing to call Jesus your best friend. The feeling of rejection and loneliness brought me to a place where I realized that Jesus should always be my best friend and that He is always there for me. Other people will disappoint you, hurt you, and leave you. Jesus will never leave you or forget about you. He loves you and cares about you so much. When things are difficult, just keep walking and trusting in Jesus. He wants to have a relationship with you, spend time with you, and speak to you through his Word and truth.

After I graduated from community college, I did not know what I wanted to do next. I was unsure what college to transfer to or if I still wanted to go to college. I was also uncertain what my major would be. So I continued to pray and asked God to guide me. He answered my prayers and led me to the University of Southern Mississippi. I was very nervous about going to a new school because a new school meant living in a new place with new roommates.

I applied too late to live in the campus dorms, so I looked for roommates on a Facebook group. I was afraid I would have another bad experience with new roommates. But the Lord knew exactly what I needed. He saw that I was afraid to go to a new place and knew I needed great friends— wonderful Christian roommates who loved the Lord and would encourage me and help me grow in my relationship with Him. Psalm 37:4 says, *Take delight in the Lord, and he will give you the desires of your heart* (NLT).

I continued to trust in the Lord as I searched for a place to live, praying and believing He would help me by providing Christian friends and roommates. The Lord did just that. He provided me with two sweet Christian roommates who lived in a house near campus.

As I am writing this, I am still unsure about what I want my college major to be. I am currently a graphic design major because I love art so much, but I am continuing to trust in the Lord to guide me where I am supposed to be. Isaiah 41:10 says, *Don't be afraid, for I am with you. Don't be discouraged, for I am your God. I will strengthen you and help you. I will uphold you with my victorious right hand* (NLT). Psalm 32:8 reminds us, *The Lord says, "I will guide you along the best pathway for your life. I will advise you and watch over you"* (NLT). The Lord will direct your steps each day. Do not be afraid of what is to come because the Lord has a plan for you, and He watches over you. He cares for you.

Jesus is the best friend that you could ever have. He is with you always and cares so much about you. Jesus is always with you and will never leave you. You are beautiful and so very loved. I want you to know that you are never alone.

Run to Jesus; He is your help, hope, and greatest friend. And He wants to spend time with you because He loves you always.

If you, like me, ever find yourself walking into a room and feeling a sudden wave of foreboding emotions, remember that Jesus is with you. He's right beside you! You are never alone; Jesus always invites you to His side—the best place anyone could ever be!

You Are Not Alone in Your Next Steps

by Katie Whitehead

I cling to you; your strong right hand holds me securely (Psalm 63:8 NLT).

Have you ever been down a zipline before? I love them. It is an amazing yet scary experience. If you have never been down a zipline before, let me take a moment to set the scene of what it's like.

First, you put on a tight harness along with ropes that will hold you up and keep you secure while riding down. As you do, you look up at this tall tower. It doesn't look too high from the ground, but when you start walking up the steps to the top, you realize how tall it really is. When you finally get to the top, you are clipped onto the rolling part of the zipline. Standing on the small platform, you look down at how far it is to the ground and start to get butterflies in your stomach from how high up you are. You think, *Oh my, I don't know if I want to do this anymore!*

"Alright, you are ready to go," says the instructor. "Just step off the platform and cross your legs."

Taking that first step off the platform isn't easy. It is terrifying! But once you take that step, you are flying! It is absolutely beautiful. You can feel the wind in your hair, and it is a joyful ride to the other side.

After taking that first step, you know that the harness and the ropes will hold you up, and it is not scary anymore because you know you are safe and secure.

Taking that first step off the zipline platform is much like having faith in Jesus when we don't know what to do next in life. You may need to activate your faith to take that first step in finding a new job or a new college major. Stepping out in faith is not easy. As you stand on that platform, there are many "what ifs" that may come to your mind. *What if I fall? What if the ropes and harness fail to hold me up?* Similarly, you may encounter those same thoughts with any new situation. *What if it doesn't work out? What if I don't succeed?*

There are many times throughout our lives when we must step out in faith, believing Jesus will hold us up.

Faith shows the reality of what we hope for; it is the evidence of things we cannot see (Hebrews 11:1 NLT).

God won't let us fall when we trust Him. He tells us in Isaiah 46:4, *I will be your God throughout your lifetime—until your hair is white with age, I have made you, and I will care for you. I will carry you along and save you* (NLT).

We only need to trust Him and take that first step, saying, "Okay, Lord, you've got this. I'm putting my trust in you. I cannot see what I am meant to do next. I cannot see what the future holds. But I know you do! You hold my future!"

For we live by believing and not by seeing (2 Corinthians 5:7 NLT).

We can put all our trust in Him. The Lord has amazing plans for your life, and He loves you deeply. He wants you to trust Him with all your life. He wants you to walk alongside Him and trust Him as He holds you up in the unknowns of life.

You are not alone! He's got you!

What first step of faith do you need to take? Are you willing to say, "Okay, Lord, I know you've got me!" Will you pray as you put all your trust and faith in Him to hold you up?

Dear Lord Jesus,

Help me today to take that first step of faith. Help me believe and trust that you are always there to hold me up, even when I don't know what to do next. Thank you for loving me and always helping me when things are hard and I don't know what to do next. You are so good to guide me. Thank you, Jesus, for always being there for me and never allowing me to take my next steps alone.

In Jesus' name, I pray. Amen.

AUBREY CARTER

Aubrey Carter grew up in Alabaster, Alabama, surrounded by friends and family who always supported her ambitious endeavors. She loves traveling, meeting new people, connecting with others, and, most of all, her Lord and Savior, Jesus Christ.

Since transferring to Mississippi State University in 2022, Aubrey has found her passion in journalism and telling stories that truly matter. In this book, Aubrey writes about the most important story in her personal life: finding joy, grace, and love through surrendering her life to Jesus Christ.

Aubrey is pursuing a degree in Digital Journalism & Broadcast and is on track to graduate in May of 2025. In lieu of this, she spends most of her days talking to community members, building relationships with those around her, and writing stories that excite her.

Since re-establishing her faith in the Lord in 2021, Aubrey believes that trusting the Lord and praying through life's ups and downs is the only way to find genuine joy and peace. She believes in the greater good of humanity and prays that each and every person will one day experience the love and grace offered through a relationship with Jesus Christ. That gives her comfort each day.

You Are Seen by the One Who Matters

by Aubrey Carter

We were born broken, wounded, and sinful. By default, it is in our nature as human beings to go about our lives doing things backward, crooked, and just completely wrong. We all yearn for acceptance, happiness, and love in our lives, but why does it often seem nearly impossible to achieve these things?

One reason may be that we devote our energy to the wrong places. The only satisfaction we will ever receive without having the love of our Lord and Savior in our hearts will be temporary and ingenuine. But if we humble ourselves and surrender our lives to Jesus Christ, we will be able to live each day with joy in our hearts and peace in our minds, despite the chaos and pain that the world brings.

> *Jesus replied: "Love the Lord your God with all your heart and with all your soul and all your mind"* (Matthew 22:37 NIV).

Love isn't something I seemed to ever lack in life. I grew up surrounded by love in a home with parents and a brother who supported me through the good and bad days. They hugged and kissed me and told me how much

I meant to them. They loved me, and I always knew it, even when I felt otherwise.

Growing up in the South, I was introduced to Jesus at a young age, or more so, introduced to religion and Christian ideology. I always believed in God and attended church here and there, but a constant nagging in my head and heart convinced me that something was missing. When I was ten years old, I asked Jesus into my heart and pranced to the front of a small church in Wakulla County, Florida, to tell the pastor I was ready to be baptized.

I was dunked under the water in front of hundreds of unknown people and was so excited to experience all the wonderful things that were about to happen. To my surprise, though, I did not feel one bit different after being raised out of that water. I was expecting to feel like a totally different person, but that wasn't the case. I was smiling ear-to-ear, but I was not totally sure what I was supposed to do after being baptized. All I knew was what other Christians had told me: to get to heaven, you have to be saved.

I may not have known a lot when I was 10, but I knew for sure I wanted to make it through those pearly gates. I knew without a doubt that Jesus was in my heart and that He loved me, but something was not connecting. I shoved the uncertainties and doubts into the back of my mind and continued life without a genuine understanding of what it means to be saved and have a relationship with Jesus Christ.

As I grew older, I found satisfaction in pleasing others and getting a pat on the head. I somehow became one of the "popular" girls in school, and I truly felt loved. I got so used to receiving constant compliments and feeling like I had a million friends.

My first year of high school began on a high. People often talk about how horrible high school was, but I thrived—until I didn't.

The more immersed in the teenage years I became, the harder I was on myself. I went from being happy with myself and who I was becoming to never feeling satisfied. I was told I was beautiful, but I didn't feel beautiful. I was told I was smart, but I didn't feel smart. People told me they were proud of me, but I didn't believe there was any reason to be proud. My confidence plummeted to the ground, but I never wanted anyone to know. I would cry myself to sleep about how I hated the way I looked, but I would turn around the next morning and smile through the hallways.

Suddenly, the love that others showed me was not enough. I didn't believe it. I wanted to be better. I needed something more. I didn't show it, though. I didn't always feel that low, but on the days I did, I made sure that I had the typical Aubrey face on. The one that everyone loved. The thought of someone disliking me made me feel ill. So, I made sure I always looked happy: I smiled, kept quiet, worked hard, dressed nice, spoke kindly, and did everything I could to continue to be accepted by others.

"If the world hates you, keep in mind that it hated me first" (John 15:18 NIV).

I had been told that I was "perfect" from a very young age, and it started consuming me. I knew I wasn't, but people convinced me that I might have been as close to perfect as possible. At first, it went to my head and built up my confidence. Eventually, it went to my head and tore me apart.

Comparison became my worst enemy. In my mind, I was never skinny enough, pretty enough, smart enough, talented enough, or good enough. I based my entire identity on what others thought and spoke of me, and I struggled every day to be what I thought everyone else wanted me to be. My insecurities took over until being "enough" was no longer possible. I still craved the approval of others, but no matter how many compliments or praises I received, I was never satisfied. My emptiness, combined with the fact I didn't realize the praise of others would never fill me up, drove me to seek attention constantly. I was convinced that if I got a certain boy's attention, was invited to the party, or was chosen for the part, I would finally be content. I wanted to be perfect. I wanted to be the best. But I was reaching for the world's unattainable standards. I was created perfect in God's image, but I was too caught up in my own desires to understand that.

> *See what great love the Father has lavished on us, that we should be called children of God! And that is what we are! The reason the world does not know us is that it did not know him* (1 John 3:1 NIV).

The more I struggled with myself, the more I felt like I was disappointing others, and the worse I felt about myself. I did things that I knew I would regret. "I'm young" and "This is what you're supposed to do as a teenager" were the excuses I made to try to convince myself that none of it was that big of a deal. Guilt slowly but surely crept up in my heart and mind, but I ignored it. At that point, I knew I had Jesus in my life, but I wanted full control. I was so caught up in the ways of this world and my own thoughts and desires that I completely put a wall up to God. I believed I was just doing what every other teenager does—and maybe I was.

> *The acts of the flesh are obvious: sexual immorality, impurity and debauchery; idolatry and witchcraft; hatred, discord, jealousy, fits of rage, selfish ambition, dissensions, factions and envy; drunkenness, orgies, and the like. I warn you, as I did before, that those who live like this will not inherit the kingdom of God* (Galatians 5:19-21 NIV).

The longer I continued down that path, the farther away I felt from my loved ones. I still tried to remain the girl everyone thought I was, but it became so much harder than it had been. I struggled to see the point of putting on a face anymore. The girl who always wanted to be seen with a smile on her face suddenly did not care as much anymore. I didn't feel like myself. No matter how hard I tried, keeping a positive attitude about anything felt almost impossible.

I felt a weight in my chest and a heaviness in my heart. I felt disconnected from my friends and family. I had a hatred toward myself for the lack of motivation I had in life. I had big dreams and aspirations, but I suddenly felt completely stuck. Part of me was still worried about what others thought of me, but I wanted to feel like myself again. I avoided situations that would lead to temptations and sin. However, I still felt lost and lonely. I felt more alone than I ever had. I couldn't pinpoint why, though. Some of my friendships began to fall apart, and suddenly, I felt like nobody cared about me or what I was doing. I was confused, sad, and lonely at times, but I knew that this season wouldn't last forever.

As my high school years ended, the decision of where to attend college was dominated by my mindset of doing what I thought others wanted me to do. In reality, very few people truly cared about what college I chose. However, I felt the need to go to a big school where I could make a name for myself, thus avoiding the whole "peaking in high school" phenomenon. I was infatuated with the idea of moving somewhere far away where nobody would know my name. I fantasized about how I could be someone totally different and how nobody would recognize me walking across campus. I had my eyes on Florida State University for a while, but I was uneasy about making a decision. I had already told so many friends and family that FSU was my dream school and how I was so excited to leave my hometown that when the time came around to make a college decision, I felt like I had no choice but to make my way to Tallahassee, Florida. I felt an overwhelming pressure to live up to some made-up standard I thought others were holding me to.

Overall, I was beyond excited about college and being on my own. I truly was ready to get out and figure out who I was supposed to be in this big world. I received my acceptance letter for Florida State, and that was it. I made my decision right then and there. I did not pray a single prayer asking God to direct me and guide me to where He wanted me to go. I had prayed hundreds of times about simply getting into FSU, but never did I stop to ask God what He wanted. God and prayer were second thoughts, and I was in the driver's seat of my life, convinced that I knew exactly where I was going.

August rolled around, and suddenly, it was time to say goodbye to my friends and family and move away to a different state. I was anticipating college to be the best years of my life—because that's what I was always told.

I got to college, settled into my little apartment with my three roommates, and quickly realized that college was not at all what it was cracked up to be. I was so excited for a do-over, but nothing went as I expected. I went from everyone knowing my name to nobody even giving me a second glance when I got to college. I thought that would make me feel free, but it felt so lonely. I went out with my roommates and other friends to the bars and clubs around town and tried to immerse myself in the typical college lifestyle. However, something felt so wrong.

The nights out quickly turned into nights sitting alone in my bed, sobbing. I gave up trying to make friends in my classes. I became introverted; I didn't even know who I was anymore. I fell into a cycle of going to bed extremely late, skipping most of my classes, going to work, and then returning home to do it all over again. I felt so invisible and out of place. It seemed everyone else was having the time of their lives, but I felt like I was just going through the motions of mine. To my friends and family, I was having the best time of my life at college. I wasn't, though. I was lonely. I was sad. I felt completely unseen.

I decided to give prayer a shot. I had been asking God to help me not feel so sad and alone, but I had again failed to ask for His will to be done in my life. I was so naïve in thinking that I knew where I needed to be and what I needed to do. God has a perfect plan for each and every one of His children. I finally decided to give Him the reins.

> *Therefore I tell you, whatever you ask for in prayer, believe that you have received it, and it will be yours* (Mark 11:24 NIV).

I began asking the Lord for peace, guidance, and grace during that time in my life.

Not long after, my grandfather, who lived in the area, invited me to a Wednesday night church service. I was more than happy to attend, as this was actually the church I had been baptized in years prior. I sat among a group of kindhearted men and women who showed me love and acceptance the moment I walked in the door.

As the service started, I was instantly intrigued and honed in on the message. I cannot say exactly what the message was about that night, but one question from the sermon stood out to me more than anything else. "Are you using prayer as a spare tire, or are you using it as your steering wheel?" I had never heard an analogy like that before, and it has occupied my mind ever since.

As I drove back to my apartment, I remember crying but feeling so safe and at peace. It finally clicked. I had finally found and reconnected the puzzle piece that had been missing since I was a child. That pastor's simple question led me to find peace and comfort, knowing Jesus has a perfect plan for me and all I have to do is surrender to Him. I did not want the sorrow, loneliness, and pain that had entered my life, and to my greatest relief, I found out that I did not have to handle it alone.

From that point on, prayer became my steering wheel. I hopped out of the driver's seat and let God take over. I prayed day in and day out, not for my desires but for God's will to be done in my life. I knew I was still at a place in my life that I wasn't sure was right for me, but I also knew God had a plan for me. I still struggled with feeling lonely, and I knew in my heart that I needed to make a change. I became so in tune with hearing God's voice because it was the only thing I wanted to listen for. I knew God was telling me I needed to enter into a new season of my life, but I was so unsure of what my next move was. I prayed when I woke up, I prayed when I walked to class, and I prayed on the way to work. I continued to pray for guidance with every moment I had.

> *Rejoice always, pray without ceasing, give thanks in all circumstances; for this is the will of God in Christ Jesus for you* (1 Thessalonians 5: 16-18 NIV).

As several months of my freshman year of college passed by, I began applying to a few other schools to transfer to. The thought of moving to a completely different school overwhelmed me, and I was worried about what other people would think if I did transfer somewhere else. However, I let the Lord's voice be the loudest. It was difficult, but I had to listen and be receptive to what God told me without being influenced by the world around me. I completely stepped away from trying to control my own life, and I let God intervene.

The puzzle pieces continued to fall into place, and I eventually found a school that ended up being a home away from home. I had to take a deep breath and step out on faith, trusting that the Lord had a plan. He did. He always does. For the first time in my life, I began to experience true joy. Happiness was an emotion that I was no stranger to, but it will never compare to the pure joy that comes from having a relationship with Jesus Christ and trusting the Lord wholeheartedly. I began to love myself and my life more than ever before. The love and mercy of Jesus Christ completely turned my life around. In no way, shape, or form is life meant to be easy. And some days are more difficult than others, but Jesus Christ is the only way. God has a perfect plan for all His children, and He will never make you feel unseen.

> *But because of his great love for us, God, who is rich in mercy, made us alive with Christ even when we were dead in transgressions—it is by grace you have been saved. And God raised us up with Christ and seated us with him in the heavenly realms in Christ Jesus, in order that in the coming ages he might show the incomparable riches of his grace, expressed in his kindness to us in Christ Jesus* (Ephesians 2:4-7 NIV).

You Are Not Alone
in Unmet Expectations

by Mendez Nelson and Lisa Tofano Hathaway

Have you ever felt let down? You know, like realizing Santa Claus and the Easter Bunny aren't real? Or when a new restaurant or movie didn't live up to the hype? We have all experienced unmet expectations that can be very disappointing. We build things up in our minds as we fantasize about what we hope will happen on the stage of our lives, usually with us at the center in the lead role. In our minds, the world revolves around us, and our needs are always met, but our experiences often produce the opposite result. What went wrong? Why are our expectations unmet? What should we do when things don't turn out how we thought they would? What are we expecting out of God, ourselves, and others? Do we always expect unfolding circumstances to make us happy?

> *Trust in the Lord with all your heart; do not depend on your own understanding. Seek his will in all you do, and he will show you which path to take* (Proverbs 3:5-6 NLT).

Trusting God can be challenging when things don't happen as we anticipate. We can even begin to doubt God and His goodness. This can cause us to take matters into our own hands, but being self-sufficient comes with a price. Leaning on our understanding can lead us astray. Our will can get in the way of God's will for us.

> *"For I know the plans I have for you," says the Lord. "They are plans for good and not for disaster, to give you a future and a hope"* (Jeremiah 29:11 NLT).

God's plans and purpose are always bigger than our own. When we lose sight of our heavenly Father's role in our lives, we can become consumed with distractions, wondering why things didn't turn out as we had hoped.

> *And we know that God causes everything to work together for the good of those who love God and are called according to his purpose for them* (Romans 8:28 NLT).

God promises to work all things for our good, even if they don't appear to be good to us at the time. We must not judge God by our circumstances. Circumstances will always change, but God never will. He can see what lies ahead. We must realize our limitations and accept that His ways and thoughts are bigger and better than our worldly desires.

> *That is why we never give up. Though our bodies are dying, our spirits are being renewed every day. For our present troubles are small and won't last very long. Yet they produce for us a glory that vastly outweighs them and will last forever! So we don't look at the troubles we can see now; rather, we fix our gaze on things that cannot be seen. For the things we see now will soon be gone, but the things we cannot see will last forever* (2 Corinthians 4:16-18 NLT).

We can learn to go to our loving Father to seek His guidance, center our lives around His will, and not become disillusioned by worldly pursuits. We are fulfilled only when we accept that we are complete in Him and know that our identity is in Him alone. Seeking His plan for our lives will satisfy us in ways we can't imagine until we experience it. He is the only one who can ever thoroughly meet our expectations—even those we didn't know we had!

The Lord sees you when you have unmet expectations. And He has the perfect plan for this long journey called life—much better than you or Santa Claus or the Easter Bunny ever could imagine!

· ·

Jean Swack

Jean Swack is a young adult who loves the Lord and her family in Christ. She is passionate about sharing the Gospel with people and hopes to see as many people come to know, love, and worship Christ as possible.

Jean was first saved in April 2020 and has been learning what it means to live her life for Jesus ever since. She has been on mission trips to Italy and Portugal with her church, and she volunteers within her church in kids' ministry and set-up as much as possible.

Jean is a Communications major at the University of Central Florida. She is also taking a program in American Sign Language Interpreting through Valencia Community College. She hopes to be an ASL Interpreter following her graduation.

She enjoys reading, going on runs, trying new things, and spending time with her friends and family. She currently works as a waitress and lives in Orlando, Florida.

SEEN IN THE DARKNESS

by Jean Swack

Despite growing up in a Christian family, I've found that it can be easy for me to take my relationship with God for granted. In my darkest days, it felt like God had completely abandoned me. For years, I struggled with depression and anxiety along with thoughts of ending my life, and it was only a matter of time until I acted on those thoughts. It seemed like God was distant and cold, unsympathetic to my pain. Yet how we feel about God does not change who He is; even though I couldn't see it at the time, God was always with me and for me. Even now, as I write this dark story, I can't help but see the light of His glory shining through it.

In 2015, when I was just short of 11 years old, life got rocky. My parents were struggling financially, so I spent many hours at home alone while they worked long hours. On top of that, my relationship with my closest friend started to fall apart. But at the time, I didn't really understand the effect all these events had on me. All I understood was that I started wanting to hurt myself.

At first, it was the mental image of plunging a knife into my stomach. The image came in a flash; unsurprisingly, it was terrifying to me. It didn't take long for other disturbing visuals to start surfing around my brain. From the start, I knew that these thoughts weren't just about injuring myself; they were about ending my life. Along with these images came cruel words telling me how no one truly liked me, that I shouldn't be allowed to be happy, and that I deserved to sit in this darkness.

In some detached sense, I knew these thoughts weren't true. Like many kids who went to Sunday school, I already knew John 3:16 by heart: *For God so loved the world, that he gave his only Son, that whoever believes in him shall not perish but have eternal life* (ESV). I didn't need to be a Bible scholar to understand this verse. It clearly shows the love God has for all believers and that we are made for life, not death. But I didn't listen; I listened to the thoughts and feelings that were so much bigger and louder than anything I had ever experienced before. I listened to what "felt" like the truth.

I didn't know other people felt this way, and I didn't know how people would react if they knew my inner dialogue. The thought of being judged or not being understood was so strong that it felt like if I tried to explain what was happening, the words would get stuck in my throat. The worst feeling imaginable was baring myself to another person, only for them not to see what I was struggling with or be told I was making mountains out of molehills.

It took years for me to finally share with another person. By then, I was almost 13 years old, and the feelings had only grown. Crying and afraid, I told my mom, "I think I might have depression." She was shocked, uncertain of what to even do with that information. I begged her to let me go to therapy. Ultimately, she agreed, thinking it would take until the end of the summer for me to start feeling better.

And so I went. But even in a therapist's office, I still couldn't find the courage to share fully. I still held back parts of the truth—the parts I felt were too ugly to let into the light. I never mentioned that I was having vivid thoughts of hurting and killing myself, and thus, no one could help me through it. As it says in James 5:16, *Therefore, confess your sins to each other and pray for each other so that you may be healed. The prayer of a righteous person is powerful and effective* (NIV). In my case, the opposite held true: by not confessing my sins and troubles to others, they couldn't speak into them, and I struggled to heal.

As summer weaned, I began to cut myself. Overcome by thoughts of ending my life, I finally tried to release some of my desire through self-harm. By the start of the school year, my parents noticed the scars. They were shocked and angry. They told my therapist, who reacted similarly. Obviously, I was not going to be done with therapy by the end of the summer.

Nighttime was always the worst for me. The thought of enduring another day always filled me with anxiety, so I would stay up late, trying to put off tomorrow for a few more hours. The problem with this, however, is that nothing good ever came from staying up that late. It was a time when I was alone with my thoughts, and looking up dark music and stories on my computer certainly didn't help. Often, nighttime would mean crying, cutting, or even panic attacks. When I was very young, my parents had taught me to pray before falling asleep, so my nights also included prayer from time to time. I would cry out to God, asking Him why he made me as I am. I wanted so badly to be different, to be someone else, in the hopes that I wouldn't feel as I felt.

Yet God did not answer my prayers. At the time, I saw this as Him abandoning me or, at the very least, ignoring my cries. Now, however, I understand that He designed me with a unique purpose—one that could not be fulfilled if I was created as anyone else. God purposefully creates each of us so we can work together in community as the body of Christ. The apostle Paul explains this in 1 Corinthians: *But now God has arranged the parts, each one of them in the body, just as He desired* (1 Corinthians 12:18 NASB). Even though I was blinded by the darkness I felt, I am so blessed to look back and see how I was never unseen by God. None of my prayers were unanswered, but not all my prayers were answered with a "yes" because His ways are higher than mine.

Unfortunately, I did not have the foresight to understand this at that time, and so I continued to struggle. In the middle of my 8th-grade year, I applied for a rigorous high school called Florida Atlantic University High School, or FAU High. This program allows students to take full-time college classes by 10th grade, and by graduation, students are three years into their bachelor's degree. I prayed daily that God would let me be accepted into this program and attend high school there. I told myself that the program seemed like a chance to get ahead of my peers, save on three years' worth of college tuition, and get a jump-start on my future. In reality, though I would not have admitted it at the time, I felt that attending FAU High would prove my worth to myself.

By the sovereign grace of the Lord, I got into the program. Though I was still depressed and had a lot of anxiety, I felt hope and excitement for my future. So, going into 9th grade, I had hopes this school would be a fresh start for me.

It didn't take long for the reality of my situation to catch up with me. I was a teenager who was suffering from undiagnosed borderline personality disorder and taking on an extremely rigorous course load. I was overwhelmed by the concept of tomorrow, and yet I was attempting to take fast-tracked classes designed to prepare 14-year-olds for the college experience. My depression and anxiety became more than I could bear. I couldn't keep up with the unrealistic expectations I had taken on and grew in hatred towards myself. By September 28, 2018, I attempted suicide for the first time.

It is by God's grace alone that I did not die that night, nor from the subsequent plans and attempts that followed. A week after that first attempt, a friend I had confided in chose (out of love) to tell the school about what I had done and that I had a desire to try again. They called me into the counselor's office, and it was not long after that I was admitted into a psychiatric hospital under the Florida Baker Act, which mandates crisis intervention and temporary detention for up to 72 hours for people in danger of harming themselves or others.

Prior to my being admitted to the hospital, my parents were not even aware that I had tried to kill myself. After years of trying to hide what I was feeling and thinking, the truth was brought into the open. It truly is, as it says in Luke: *Nothing is covered up that will not be revealed, or hidden that will not be known. Therefore whatever you said in the dark shall be heard in the light, and what you have whispered in the private rooms shall be proclaimed on the housetops* (Luke 12:2-3 ESV).

Sadly, my desire to end my life did not end there. From 2018 until the end of 2019, I was Baker Acted six times, either for admitting that I wanted to commit suicide or for attempting again. It was clear I was not fully trying to recover since I had placated the treatment team to get through one hospitalization, only to end up at another. The truth was, I didn't want to recover. I wanted to give up.

Somewhere around this time, in the blur of treatment and attempts, I found Psalm 6. It reads, *Have mercy on me, Lord, for I am faint; heal me, Lord, for my bones are in agony. My soul is in deep anguish. How long, Lord, how long?* (Psalm 6:2-3 NIV). I sobbed reading these words. Very few words had come close to describing what I was feeling as the phrase *my bones are in agony*. What I couldn't comprehend was how David still rejoices at the end of the psalm: *Away from me, all you who do evil, for the Lord has heard my weeping. The Lord has heard my cry for mercy; the Lord accepts my prayer* (Psalm 6:8-9 NIV). I wanted to believe that the Lord could hear my cry and accept my prayer in this way. That I could rejoice in the same way David does.

In December 2019, I was Baker Acted for the sixth time. After, my therapist put my application for a residential program into motion. On January 2, 2020, I was admitted to Sandy Pines Residential Treatment Center.

Even while I was in that facility, the suicide attempts didn't stop. Every night, I prayed that God would kill me in my sleep and I wouldn't have to wake up again. It was as if once I had finally given into the thoughts of death, the whole notion consumed me. The Bible depicts this well in Romans 1, where it states, *And since they did not see fit to acknowledge God, God gave them up to a debased mind to do what ought not to be done* (Romans 1:28 ESV). Though I had convinced myself that God was not acknowledging me, it was ultimately me who was not acknowledging Him. I chose to believe the lies over the truth of God's Word. Lies that included me being unworthy of life and me knowing how I should be made or who should live and die better than the King of the universe does. Though I may never fully understand why I struggled the way I did (and sometimes still do) with emotions, I do know His ways are still higher than my own (Isaiah 55:8-9), and it is not my place to tell my Creator how I should be made (Jeremiah 18:1-6, Isaiah 45:9).

> *"For my thoughts are not your thoughts, neither are your ways my ways," declares the Lord. "As the heavens are higher than the earth, so are my ways higher than your ways and my thoughts than your thoughts"* (Isaiah 55:8-9 NIV).

"Like clay in the hand of the potter, so are you in my hand" (Jeremiah 18:6 NIV).

"Woe to those who quarrel with their Maker, those who are nothing but potsherds among the potsherds on the ground. Does the clay say to the potter, 'What are you making?' Does your work say, 'The potter has no hands'?" (Isaiah 34:9 NIV).

In my own sinfulness and pain, I continued trying to end my life from within the facility. As God had done so many times before, He again stepped in to save me from myself. As I continued to try to harm myself, the facility acted to try to protect me from myself as well. I was placed on bathroom restriction (meaning I had to be watched anytime I used the restroom because I couldn't be trusted). Eventually, they sent me to another Baker Act facility. I was desperate and hopeless; all I could see ahead of me was darkness.

In order to be transported from Sandy Pines to the Baker Act facility and back, a third-party transportation system, somewhat like Lyft or Uber but for professional uses only, drove me. On the ride returning to Sandy Pines, I talked gingerly with the man driving the car. While we made small talk, he casually mentioned that he was Christian. I responded that I was Christian as well, to which he boldly but gently asked why I was doing these things to myself if I was a Christian. I admitted that I believed in Jesus Christ, but I had no faith in Him. For so many years, I'd understood that God was there, but I couldn't see Him or feel Him in my life. I said that people had told me He is loving, but all I felt was that He was a God I could never satisfy. Then the driver told me about grace—that God offers us free grace as a gift.

Receiving God's love and goodness is not dependent on what we do but is something He gives us because of His Son, Jesus, and the price He paid for us on the cross. The driver reminded me that Jesus has already paid the price for all my sins and mistakes; all I have to do is believe in Him and accept the gift of grace.

Though I had heard about God's grace all my life, something struck me differently in this conversation. It's like it says in 1 Corinthians 2:14 (ESV): *The natural person does not accept the things of the Spirit of God, for they are folly to him, and he is not able to understand them because they are spiritually discerned.* In other words, my brain could not comprehend these things until the Spirit of God gave me the ability to. By the end of that car ride, the driver led me through the salvation prayer.

All the symptoms I experienced having borderline personality disorder didn't disappear as soon as that prayer ended. But thankfully, the will to kill myself did. I still fantasized about suicide and still struggled with overwhelming emotions. Yet I didn't attempt again from that moment on. I finally started to share the ugly truth—all the ways I really felt and thought—without censoring them to make me sound less sinful than I was. Little did I know the incredible relief I would feel from that.

Since May 5, 2020, I have not made a single attempt on my life or even self-harmed. By June 29, I was released from Sandy Pines, and God has only continued to grow and restore me since then. Not only did He save me by dying on the cross, but He saved me from myself.

The further I get from this time in my life, the more I can truly see that I was not the one who orchestrated my way through this, but that it was God who brought me through it. Not long after returning home, I started to rely on scripture to help me through dark moments as they came. Scripture like Philippians 4:13 (NIV), *I can do all things through him [Christ] who gives me strength,* gave me courage during panic attacks and when suicidal thoughts resurfaced. The more I read from the Bible, the more my mind was renewed by it.

Today, I could not be more grateful for what the Lord has done in my life and the new life I now have in Christ. I still am sinful, and I still struggle with dark thoughts from time to time, but it's nothing like what I walked through before.

Praise be to God that I no longer walk in darkness but in light!

You Are Not Alone in Your Anxiety

by Mendez Nelson and Lisa Tofano Hathaway

The word anxiety is so prevalent today; so many people experience the symptoms of anxiety and worry. It can consume our lives in ways that can be crippling. We feel overwhelmed by all the decisions and the fast pace of society today. We are constantly bombarded with the pressures of life, often exacerbated by social media. It is not uncommon for our minds to create a narrative we cannot live up to, which can be debilitating.

But freedom from anxiety is possible. God wants to walk with us to help us win this battle. In Philippians, Paul gives the best advice: *Don't worry about anything; instead, pray about everything. Tell God what you need and thank him for all he has done. Then you will experience God's peace, which exceeds anything we can understand. His peace will guard your hearts and minds as you live in Christ Jesus* (Philippians 4:6-7 NLT).

This scripture is powerful. It tells us not to worry about anything. Ask God for what you need and continue to thank Him for all He has done. Gratitude combats anxiety. Gratitude and anxiety cannot coexist together. Studies show that gratitude helps train your brain to notice and appreciate the little things in life and, in doing so, shifts your life experience tremendously. Gratitude can increase your happiness and well-being, life satisfaction, and overall health while decreasing what we want less of—like anxiety, depression, and anger.

> *Then Jesus said, "Come to me, all of you who are weary and carry heavy burdens, and I will give you rest. Take my yoke upon you. Let me teach you, because I am humble and gentle at heart, and you will find rest for your souls. For my yoke is easy to bear, and the burden I give you is light." (Matthew 11:28-30 NLT).*

God wants our souls to rest in Him and be free from the world's anxieties. But we know this is a daily and sometimes minute-by-minute choice for us. We will face anxieties and worries as we walk through this life. God never promised us this would be an easy road and journey, but He did promise us He would be with us.

> *"I have told you these things, so that in Me you may have [perfect] peace. In the world you have tribulation and distress and suffering, but be courageous [be confident, be undaunted, be filled with joy]; I have overcome the world." [My conquest is accomplished, My victory abiding.] (John 16:33 AMP).*

One thing we can be sure of is that the God of the universe does not want His children to walk in the bondage that anxiety and worry can bring. He has equipped us with the tools to fight against the enemy. But again, it is a choice. Sometimes, we might not see a way out of this struggle and feel captivated by the anxiety, but continually thanking God for the smallest of things in our lives can bring freedom.

> *When my anxious thoughts multiply within me, Your comforts delight me* (Psalm 94:19 AMP).

God's comfort is real and tangible. Keep your eyes open to see His hand on your life, even if it is in small ways. He constantly wants you to come to Him and ask for His help. God longs and desires to be a part of every aspect of our lives, the big and the tiny things. Nothing is impossible for God. Take heart that you do not have to live with anxiety controlling your life.

Be thankful in all things and know God sees you and what you are walking through.

. . . .

Olivia Whiteside

Olivia Whiteside is currently a student at Texas A&M University in College Station, pursuing her bachelor's degree in accounting and her masters degree in supply chain management.

Olivia comes from a family with nine siblings—two biological and seven step-siblings. She grew up in Cypress, Texas, playing soccer and clarinet throughout high school. She is passionate about spreading positivity to the people around her and making sure that everyone feels included, noticed, and encouraged.

Olivia loves being outside, playing sports with friends and just being in nature. She grew up in the church and has been going through the journey of making her faith her own since going to college. Her favorite Bible verses are Jeremiah 29:11 and Luke 12:27-28.

Olivia is excited to continue deepening her faith and growing her relationship with God to confidently step into the plans set in store for her.

FULLY KNOWN AND FULLY LOVED

By Olivia Whiteside

Our high school and college years are a time of transition and growth. While some people can point to a specific life event that changed them or tell you they followed five easy steps to become a better version of themselves, I can't do either. But I can say that throughout my college career, God continually moved in my life—even when I couldn't see Him and most certainly in ways I didn't even know I needed. He saw me.

Imposter syndrome is something that I have struggled with throughout my life but never really recognized until I got to college. Throughout high school, I thought I was just shy; thoughts of being a fraud exposed my anxiety and insecurity. I belonged to groups and teams and *called* myself "a part of them," but I never felt good enough about myself to actually consider myself an integral part of anything. I constantly felt unworthy and undeserving to be in the places I was in.

I was on the soccer team and in the band, and like many high schoolers, I allowed my activities to determine my identity. But the whole time, I felt like an imposter—unworthy and undeserving to be there, so I always felt out of place. This left me unsure of myself and constantly looking to others for validation. I was a people pleaser with imposter syndrome—not a fun combo. There was always a voice in the back of my mind telling me that it was a mistake I was wherever I was. Inside, I heard over and over, *Nobody wants you here. You aren't good enough. And You don't belong. It left me feeling alone and unseen.*

I grew up in a Christian household where we went to church every Sunday. I was at church every opportunity I got—my real community was there, including my best friends. I relied on that community, but even there, I felt somewhat like an imposter. Like I wasn't doing enough or didn't have enough of a relationship with God. I would look around and see what everyone was doing and the faith they claimed to have, feeling like my relationship with God didn't even compare to theirs. But that was the problem. I was looking to everyone else's relationships with God to judge mine. It wasn't that I thought about the quality of my relationship with God; it was that I compared our relationships side by side. But I didn't just compare everyone else's *true* relationships with God; I compared what I perceived those relationships to be. I wasn't in everyone else's minds or hearts; I just assumed and *perceived* that everyone else had an amazingly perfect relationship with God and thought mine should be the same, but I knew it wasn't (not to mention a "perfect" relationship is not possible on this earth). So I felt out of place.

Along with this misplacement in the church, every time I stepped into my high school, I felt unsure of myself and like I didn't belong. I was instantly scared to talk to anyone and felt out of place. Thoughts constantly raced through my head like, *Don't talk to them; they won't want to talk to you. Everyone here thinks you shouldn't be here. None of these people really want to talk to you; they are just being polite and will talk behind your back when you leave.* These thoughts caused me to second-guess everything I did, fearing nobody would like me. I was never myself; instead, I was a version of myself I thought everyone wanted me to be. I was scared to have an opinion that people didn't agree with and scared to say the wrong thing because, if I did, I wouldn't be of any value to them. Life was so tiring, and I didn't even realize it because that was what I had always known. Looking back, I can see these thoughts were lies from the enemy. But while I was there, they were just simple lies that I believed as truths without a second thought.

The beginning of college brought new worries and questions about my identity. If I didn't have band, soccer, or other things to mark my identity, who was I? I knew all the typical Christian answers: "I am a child of God." "I am loved by Him." "I am fearfully and wonderfully made." But I didn't live like I actually believed them.

Meeting new people in college was awesome, in theory. I had the opportunity to start fresh, and "the quiet and shy Olivia that people knew in high school" wasn't who I had to be anymore. I could be myself, but now the new question was posed: *Who am I?*

During my first semester at college, I was learning who I was and how to be myself. It was hard. I had a new confidence, knowing I could finally try to be myself, but then I constantly fell back into the trap of people pleasing and wanting everyone to perceive me well and like me. Many of my initial relationships were formed based on my efforts to be what I thought others wanted me to be. I was learning to be more of my authentic self, but I was still portraying a version of myself that I thought the person in front of me would like. I still had thoughts of not belonging and that everyone around me didn't want me to be there because they considered me undeserving.

I constantly wondered: *What if they don't like me? What if I'm not funny enough to be around them? What if I'm too quiet? What if I'm too loud? What if I don't talk enough? What if I talk too much? What if they think I'm fat? What if they think I'm ugly? What if they feel like I'm imposing and don't actually want me there? What if they are all annoyed every time I speak? What if I'm not needed? What if they just act like they want me here but actually don't?*

It was exhausting and so anxiety-inducing trying to go through day to day because I was constantly tied up in the fact that everyone needed to like me, but at the same time, I was 100 percent certain when I walked into a room that nobody wanted me there. It was an impossible game to win. My mind would only be satisfied, and I would only feel "worthy" when everyone around me liked me. However, I also wouldn't believe that anyone liked me. These never-ending thoughts were lies straight from the devil, but I accepted them as truths.

This continued throughout my first year of college, but then I started to see a shift happen. I began feeling more included in the groups I was in and more equipped to be where I was. This shift did not occur due to my actions but because of where I began to find my identity. I had stopped trying to get the approval and validation of others and began to understand my worth and value in Christ. Immediately, I started to feel more confident and secure in my relationships. I wasn't as afraid to mess up or show the imperfect side of myself, or any part of myself for that matter. I felt more and more free as time went on. I can confidently say that some of this came from finding a solid relationship with God that I could call my own, but ALL of it was due to God seeing me where I was and revealing the lies that had infiltrated my life.

I finally recognized that so much of what hindered me were all lies from the enemy. None of them were so outlandish that I could recognize them as lies at the time—the devil is tricky. He knows how to heap little things on us that add up. *The serpent was the shrewdest of all the wild animals the Lord God had made* (Genesis 3:1 NLT). I believed his lies for so long that I never even second-guessed them. They had been impressed into my identity and were the reason for who I was at the time. These all contributed to my imposter syndrome, leaving me thinking I was unseen and alone.

I learned that there is a truth that is infinitely better and more beautiful for each of the lies I believed.

- *Lie Number One was, "I need other people's validation to be worthy." The Truth is, "Who I am in Christ makes me worthy."*

My imposter syndrome was most prevalent when I tried to find my worth in others and what they thought of me. I sought validation and identity through the people around me instead of who I knew I was in Christ. Galatians 1:10 says, *For am I now seeking the approval of man, or of God? Or am I trying to please man? If I were still trying to please man, I would not be a servant of Christ* (ESV). When I first read this verse, it made me uncomfortable. It sounded harsh, and I didn't like Paul speaking so candidly. I wanted something to build me up and make me feel good, and this just called me out. But the more I sat on this verse, the more I saw the truth and the beauty in it. We cannot serve two masters, and we cannot please God and man at the same time. But isn't that a wonderful thing? This life is not ours, so isn't it so much better that we have the opportunity to spend it serving a God who is perfect and loving instead of serving a man who is imperfect and unreliable?

When I spent my time interacting with others, focusing on myself and how they viewed me, it only led to constant anxiety, overthinking, and feeling out of place. I was so worried about how I was being perceived that I wasn't actually building relationships or even being myself. I was only a shell of the person I thought others wanted me to be. Everything changes when we know our identity in Christ and our focus shifts from "How do others see me?" to "How do others see God through me?"

- *Lie Number Two was, "Nobody wants me anywhere or thinks I deserve to be here." The Truth is, "God always positions me perfectly."*

This lie most significantly contributed to my mindset of people-pleasing. Every room I walked into, I automatically thought everyone disliked me, didn't want me there, or thought I was an inconvenience. These beliefs are crazy when I say them out loud (or write them down), but I truly believed them and never questioned if they were true. Not even my friends knew I was having these thoughts. I was so convinced that people around me didn't want me there that I would put on any air or do anything to convince them otherwise. Realizing this as a lie took a long time to process. I had been projecting my insecurities and doubts onto others because it was a lot easier than dealing with the fact that I was the one who couldn't accept myself. It was a lot easier to count myself out from the beginning rather than have hope that others would like me and then be wrong and embarrassed.

One really cool thing about God revealing this lie to me is how He not only put His truth into my life, but He also proved it. Recently, I ran into somebody from my high school I had never really talked to that much. Reverting to my high school mindset, I acted like I didn't see them and kept walking—because why would they want to talk to me? However, they went out of their way to say hi and see how I was doing. We didn't talk for long, but it was fun just catching up. It was just a cool way God affirmed all He has been teaching me. I was ready to walk by them and not acknowledge my past, but God saw me and gave me the chance to redeem my past and step into a new space.

I also now understand that the lie that nobody wants me around makes everything about what I deserve and how I am viewed. But circumstances aren't all about me. In reality, we are all worthy of nothing. Everything we have is from the grace of God. So, if God has put me somewhere, who am I to say that the plan of the perfect Creator of the universe is wrong and that I shouldn't be there? It's not my plan, not your plan, or the plan of the person I am trying to gain approval from, but our loving and perfect Father's plan.

- *Lie Number Three was, "I have to look to other people for permission to be myself." The Truth is, "I am a child of God; I can rest in who I am in Him."*

I was always looking to everyone else to see what my options were. I was scared to be something people didn't like, so I decided I would just be a mix of everyone I saw. I felt like I didn't have permission to be anything I didn't already see in people, even if that wasn't me.

God has been showing me that just because someone hasn't gone before me in life and done something doesn't mean that that option is closed off. Just because I haven't seen someone else do something doesn't mean I can't do it. If anything, God has given me an invitation to try something new and step into His plan for me.

This truth frees me to embark on little things, like wearing a funky pair of sunglasses I've never seen anyone else wear, and big things, like choosing a major that I don't know anyone in or pursuing a job I haven't heard of anyone else having. God has given me my life. And He calls me to honor Him with all I do. I can trust where He leads me; I don't have to worry about what anyone else says. God Himself has put desires and dreams in my heart, and He put them there for a reason. The holy and perfect God made me in His image, and He does not make mistakes.

We are each called to be who God calls us to be.

Now that I recognize these truths and can identify the lies I was believing, I am so much more secure in myself and my identity in Christ. How others see me is no longer important to me; it is only important how others see God through me.

With this new perspective that God has slowly shifted me towards, I wish I could tell you that I have it all figured out and that I am secure in my identity every day I wake up. But the reality of the situation is that this will be something that I have to remind myself to believe and acknowledge constantly. I consciously choose to believe it each time I wake up. I sometimes fall back into hearing the old lies, but then I remind myself that I have a loving God who is there to see me where I am, pick me right back up again, and remind me of the truths and the identity I have in Him.

The Truth is: I am fully known, fully loved, and fully seen by God. And as His child, so are you.

You Are Not Alone in Suffering

by Mendez Nelson and Lisa Tofano Hathaway

Suffering can be intertwined in our stories throughout our lives. No one is immune or exempt from hard times or unexpected afflictions, which can often be life-altering. Following Jesus is not always easy, especially in times of trouble. But you are never alone.

There is fullness of God when we walk hand in hand with Jesus, but when we do, we may mistakenly think that because God is good, we will not go through trouble and hardship in our lives. As a result, unexpected afflictions can cause us to feel far from God and leave us with many unanswered questions. *Why did this happen? Why did God let this happen to me?*

If you have experienced suffering in your story, God sees you and has not left you. He is sitting with you in the valley. Sometimes, the valley can feel lonely and trick us into believing we will never escape the depths of pain and anguish. But God promises that He will carry us through the valley, and all we experience will help us develop strength and perseverance as we cling to Him.

> *Not only so, but we also glory in our sufferings because we know that suffering produces perseverance, perseverance, character, and character, hope* (Romans 5:3-4 NIV).

Suffering in circumstances God has allowed us to walk through can be difficult. But God promises He will be with us in these times of trouble. We prefer to bypass hard times or immediately be delivered from them, but God wants us to grow in our relationship with Him during our hard times of affliction.

The Oxford Languages Dictionary defines suffering as "the state of undergoing pain, distress, or hardship." We can feel like the victim in our story when we experience pain, distress, or hardships. God sees the bigger picture and wants us to become the victor in our journey. It takes courage to press through trials and not be destroyed.

We are hard pressed on every side, but not crushed; perplexed, but not in despair; persecuted, but not abandoned; struck down, but not destroyed (2 Corinthians 4:8-9 NIV).

When we are on the valley floor, we can be flooded with emotions of defeat, fear, abandonment—you fill in the blank. We cannot fathom the work that God does in the valley. If we are open to Him, He shapes and molds our hearts, preparing us for future service to Him. We begin to see how faithful He is and are enabled to proclaim how faithful He will be.

When my soul is in the dumps, I rehearse everything I know of you (Psalm 42: 6a MSG).

This verse clearly shows us that we can rehearse everything we know of God. Rehearse is a powerful word because we play it like a movie over and over in our minds. This creates a picture of how faithful our God is.

God sees the end from the beginning and will lift us out of the valley so we can see all He has planned for us. Our suffering has such a purpose, and He will always guide us. And He will empower us to shine His light and be living proof of how He moves and works. Our hope lies in the truth that God is with us no matter what.

We must choose to worship in the valley and through the suffering. We must choose to allow our minds to rehearse all the good we know of God and not focus on the negative of our situation. My friend, He sees you in your suffering and is constantly there with you.

> *When you go through deep waters, I will be with you. When you go through rivers of difficulty, you will not drown. When you walk through the fire of oppression, you will not be burned up; the flames will not consume you* (Isaiah 43:2 NLT).

. . . .

MICAH MORGAN

Micah Morgan is passionate about deepening her relationship with Jesus and learning to love as He did.

Micah found the redemptive love of Christ in her early years of college. Therefore, she is glad to share her story and encourage others to place their hope in Jesus, too.

Micah is a wife to Bryant and a student at Mississippi College, where she is studying English, psychology, and art. She hopes to use what she is learning to help others.

Micah loves learning, journaling, making things, nature, and spending time with her husband.

She and her husband (along with their two pets) reside in central Mississippi, where she was born and raised.

Seen & Hidden in His Shadow

by Micah Morgan

Being in the shadows...

What comes to mind when you hear the term "shadow?" You may imagine darkness, gloominess, or even a scary place. While we often associate the light as revealing, we tend to picture shadows as places where we can cower to avoid exposure. Furthermore, to "live in someone's shadow" usually denotes receiving little notice or value due to the greatness of another. Often, the shadows within this world give us a false sense of security, serving as places of temporary shelter rather than permanent refuge. However, what if there is a shadow where we can find lasting refuge and security? What if there is a shadow in which we can be hidden in protection yet completely seen and valued at the same time? I would submit to you that there is only one shadow in which we can find all these things—His name is Jesus.

When I was a little girl, my mom often referred to me as her "little shadow." There was no use in debating it on my end, as I knew it was true. I wanted to go everywhere she went. When Mom would play the grand piano in our home, I would quietly claim a seat right next to her on the edge of the bench. I would watch her so intently as her fingers stroked the keys and made the most beautiful melody I had ever heard. Honestly, I think she could have played horribly, and I still might have liked it. That is because I simply loved her.

Because I loved her, I wanted to be with her and match her every step. I was proud to be her shadow. And because I was often with her, my love for her only grew.

Usually, that is what happens when we follow someone closely, isn't it? We follow someone because we like them, and the more time we spend with them, the more our love for them grows. I wonder if you can relate. Have you ever followed someone so closely? Have you ever followed someone because you liked them, and yet the more time you spent with them, the more your love for them grew? Maybe you can fill in the blank with a family member or a mentor you look up to. Or, possibly, that is how you would describe your relationship with Jesus.

Sitting by my mom's side at the piano was just one setting where I followed her intimately. My beautiful piano-playing mother also practiced dentistry. After school in the afternoons, my brothers and I would often stay at her office with her until she finished her work. Even there, I would watch her closely as she tediously worked with her hands and treated her patients with such kindness and care. *I want to be just like her when I grow up,* I would think to myself. There I was, watching her closely and, in return, growing in adoration of her.

Another random childhood memory that has somehow stuck with me all these years looks like this: A young, blonde, pig-tailed girl riding her bicycle up and down her long driveway, saying out loud to herself, "My momma is the kindest. My momma is best," over and over again—because I truly believed it. I have a phenomenal dad whom I love, and growing up, I had several good friends, yet there was something special about the relationship my mom and I shared. I was proud to be "her shadow," and I believed I would always feel safe, accepted, and treasured in her presence. With tears in my eyes, however, I must admit that those memories, along with others like them, are merely the highlights in a complicated story of a slowly fading relationship with the woman I loved most: my mom. Even still, something so tragic in my life would be a catalyst for desperation, ultimately pointing me toward a Savior who would change everything for me.

My parents divorced when I was young, and a few years later, my mom slowly became more absent in my life. It was devastating for the little pig-tailed girl once known as her "shadow." Looking back now, I can see that every time I felt that she didn't show up for me, the feeling of being unloved and unseen developed deeper roots. I blamed myself for my mom's absence, assuming it was because I was not enough. With each sting of betrayal, my self-worth decreased. As much as I desired things to change for the better or return to "normal," the relationship I had once known quickly faded, leaving me feeling helpless. Little did I know, my mom was fighting her own battles of addiction and past traumas, and while I still desired her presence and support in my life, I realize now that she was struggling to help herself. However, as her presence helplessly faded from my life, my source of security and worth also began to vanish. While I believed in God, I had not yet known Him as my shelter or safe place.

Maybe you have not literally followed a person around to the extent that my kid-self did, but we can all relate to the feeling of wanting to be with someone because they make us feel something: loved, safe, comforted, cared for, seen, valued—add whatever you want to that list. I'd also take a gamble that most of us have experienced the harsh yet sometimes inevitable reality of losing touch with someone whom we desired to be close to always.

Think for just a moment if you can. I'm sorry if this hurts. When you lost that person, I wonder, did your sense of security, value, or identity also seem to slip away? You might even still feel a slight sting of pain, just as I do. That is okay. Before diving deeper into this journey of my testimony that covers both love and loss, let me foreshadow what I have found: There IS a safe place, a shadow that never shifts, fades, or leaves you lonely. His name is Jesus, and in Him, we can find the love and security that our souls often wander to find here on earth.

Paul boldly writes in the New Testament, *Follow me as I follow Christ* (1 Corinthians 11:1 MEV). Paul's love for Christ urged him to follow Him, and the more time Paul abided in Jesus, the more passionate about Jesus he became. In fact, Paul's testimony as described in the New Testament of the Bible is a picture of what it looks like to meet Jesus, be overwhelmed by His love and mercy, turn from your past, and choose to follow Him for the rest of your life. Paul took the Gospel personally, as he said, *I have been crucified with Christ. It is no longer I who live, but Christ who lives in me. And the life I now live in the flesh, I live by faith in the Son of God, who loved me and gave himself up for me* (Galatians 2:20 ESV). When Paul fully understood that Jesus died for him on the cross, he allowed Jesus to radically transform his life. He chose to make his home and find his purpose in Christ. I pray that you and I choose to do the same.

The security found in Christ Jesus is not just for those with broken families or those who have faced abandonment. The Bible says in 2 Samuel 22:31 that *He shields ALL who take refuge in Him* (NIV, emphasis added). The unfortunate reality of this fleeting life is that even if you have great parents or a phenomenal marriage, those relationships are still not places of unfailing security. As humans, we let each other down even when we do not mean to. That is why we so desperately need a Savior.

While I sometimes wish the reality that we fail one another were not true, it also offers comfort. After all, why would we want to put our hope in something or someone who is only temporary? Scripture talks about our lives on earth being like a vapor, here today and gone tomorrow. On the contrary, God is eternal, and His love is everlasting. Furthermore, our souls have craved His perfect love from the day we were born. We do not have to wait until we get to heaven to experience His love and security—it has been made available to us through Jesus Christ. When Jesus went to the cross, he paid for *all* our shortcomings that separated us from God so that we could experience a heavenly love and relationship with God our Father both now and forever.

When we give our lives to Christ, we can rest in His shadow. Psalm 91:1 speaks of this: *Whoever dwells in the shelter of the Most High will rest in the shadow of the Almighty* (NIV).

That verse began to resonate with me during college when I was far from a place of rest. I had gone to college full of nerves, excitement, and expectations. Without my mom's presence, my high school years had been rough, and I was ready for a fresh start. However, my first year of college was far different than I planned. Within the first few weeks, I experienced two sudden losses, my mom's condition was worsening, and I was living a half-in-half-out life with Christ, fighting an inward tug-of-war battle between chasing worldly pleasures and following Christ. Where would I find rest for my weary soul?

The period of my life in which I thought I'd be "thriving" and taking advantage of my newfound freedom was actually when I discovered the brevity of life and began to ponder my purpose more than ever. I started to wonder if the hard things that had happened in my life, such as my family separating and losing the version of my mom I once knew, could serve some purpose other than the pain and scars they left me. I clung to that hope and decided to surrender my life fully to Christ. I had experienced the devastation that resulted from placing my security and value in the hands of others, so I knew I had nothing to lose by placing my security in Jesus. I slowly began departing from the worldly lifestyle I had lived and deepening my relationship with Jesus in an attempt to discover my purpose and identity through Him.

By sophomore year, I had moved to a different city, transferred schools, and joined the cheer team at my new university. I was undergoing significant changes, yet I was passionate about my fresh pursuit of a relationship with Christ. However, I also lacked a community of believers, which led to feelings of loneliness and doubt. Still battling insecurities and the lies I believed about myself derived from the betrayal I experienced, fear and anxiety took their toll on me. It was then that I read Psalm 91:1 and wondered if it could be true that I could find rest for my anxious soul in the Lord.

For the first time, I intentionally spent time with the Lord every day, and just like I had with my mom, I began to adore Him more and more. I started to crave the time I spent in His Word, praying and simply talking to Him in the quiet place. I began to speak to Him like a friend for the first time, and I gradually learned what it meant to dwell in His shelter and find rest in His shadow. Unlike other shadows in which I had longed to dwell and find security, this one was different. It was immovable and truly secure.

Sometimes, I wonder if God needed to bring me to a place of loneliness and desperation to help me see that He is "the God who sees me" and the only one who can fill my otherwise insatiable heart. Since that time, God has not only been my refuge, but He has also gently lifted me to my feet, gradually healing the pain from my past. He has worked through a loving community and counselors in my life who have helped me unlearn the lies I believed about myself caused by the trauma of losing my mom. I have learned that my family did not fall apart, nor did my mom betray me because I was not enough. I am still learning that my value was never meant to be tied to security in other people. Years after experiencing the initial sting of betrayal, I am learning to replace the lies I believed about myself with the truth about who I am in Christ.

The wound of my past cut deep, so the healing is quite a journey, yet it is worth it and made possible by Jesus. No matter where you are, It is okay to ask for help, and it is essential to show yourself grace and patience as you work towards healing after experiencing betrayal. Before you were created, Christ believed *you were enough* for Him to leave heaven, come down to a sin-stricken world, face betrayal by people he loved wholeheartedly, and die a lonely, brutal death that He did not deserve—all to know and love you.

Jesus sympathizes with us. *For we do not have a high priest [Jesus] who is unable to sympathize with our weaknesses, but one who in EVERY respect has been tempted as we are, yet without sin* (Hebrews 4:15 ESV, emphasis added). God does not only see us, but He also feels compassion towards us, which is why He does not leave us the same after we find Him. When we surrender to Christ, His love gradually begins to redeem our lives.

When I was younger, I did not fully grasp the reality of God's redeeming love. Instead, I spent so much of my adolescence living in a place of hurt and insecurity from the betrayal I had experienced. Yet today, while I realize I will always feel sorrow from my loss, I can testify that through God's mercy and grace, I have found hope that I can live redeemed and secure in Christ. I do not have to live fearing betrayal because my security is now rooted and protected in Christ.

Through my journey, I have learned that when hard things happen to us, either intentionally or not, we process them in some fashion. For most of my life I processed the betrayal I experienced from my mom's absence all alone, which led me to believe the lie that I was not enough and a fear of experiencing betrayal again. I tried to conceal my brokenness, afraid to let others into my pain. However, by the grace of God, I have found a better way to process the hurt I have experienced: allowing the Holy Spirit and a community of believers to point me to the hope found in the Gospel of Jesus. When the perils of this life lead us to feelings of hopelessness, the

Gospel will remind us of our hope in Jesus. The Gospel will remind us that Jesus has *compassion* for His children and gave Himself to show us the love our hearts desire and yearn for—the love we cannot find here on earth without Him. While this is not an absolute remedy for pain, this wisdom has become so precious to me in moments of deep sorrow.

So let me ask: Are you living from a place of hurt or hope?

I pray you are living from a place of hope, but if you aren't, I pray that you take whatever step necessary to welcome God into those wounded places so you can truly find rest in Him. This does not mean that you reject your emotions. On the contrary, process with the Holy Spirit, other believers, or counselors as you allow your deepest emotions to catapult you into the truth of how much He loves and values you. So that despite what life has dealt you or what you may encounter, your identity as a *chosen* and *dearly loved* (Colossians 3:12-14) child of God will never be snatched from you. Let God's shadow of mercy and love and protection be where you dwell. Trust Him with your pain, and run to His secure fortress. Abide there and find rest for your soul. Make your home with Him in this secret place. Mourn there and rejoice there. It is safe. Better yet, you can spend eternity there with Him. Why wait?

My story is not yet complete, as it is still unfolding in sometimes beautiful and, other times, painfully harsh realities. Even still, I share my story of indescribable loss to remind myself and others of my hope. The hope that, even in the presence of my deepest pain, there is tender love awaiting me in the shadow of my Savior, Jesus Christ. In Jesus, my weary soul has found rest.

And it is in His shadow that you are protectively hidden, yet lovingly seen, too.

Whoever dwells in the shelter of the Most High
    will rest in the shadow of the Almighty.
I will say of the Lord, "He is my refuge and my fortress,
    my God, in whom I trust."
Surely he will save you
    from the fowler's snare
    and from the deadly pestilence.
He will cover you with his feathers,
    and under his wings you will find refuge;
    his faithfulness will be your shield and rampart.
You will not fear the terror of night,
    nor the arrow that flies by day,
nor the pestilence that stalks in the darkness,
    nor the plague that destroys at midday.
A thousand may fall at your side,
    ten thousand at your right hand,
    but it will not come near you.
You will only observe with your eyes
    and see the punishment of the wicked.
If you say, "The Lord is my refuge,"
    and you make the Most High your dwelling,
no harm will overtake you,
    no disaster will come near your tent.
For he will command his angels concerning you
    to guard you in all your ways;
they will lift you up in their hands,
    so that you will not strike your foot against a stone.
You will tread on the lion and the cobra;
    you will trample the great lion and the serpent.
"Because he loves me," says the Lord, "I will rescue him;
    I will protect him, for he acknowledges my name.
He will call on me, and I will answer him;
    I will be with him in trouble,
    I will deliver him and honor him.
With long life I will satisfy him
    and show him my salvation."

(Psalm 91 NIV)

You Are Not Alone in Fear

by Mendez Nelson and Lisa Tofano Hathaway

What is your biggest fear? Is it being:

- alone
- rejected
- abandoned
- a failure
- left out
- isolated
- not included
- not good enough
- not belonging
- or not fitting in?

We all have a basic human need to be accepted. God did not create us to be alone but created us for community. In community we have relationships, which can bring conflict, sometimes making us feel unseen and rejected. This can produce fear because we have a core desire to want to belong. Fear can cause us to hide from others and even God. When we feel rejected or abandoned by others, we tend to do things to fit in and feel accepted. Trying to do these things can go against what God has for us, causing Satan to attack our core need for acceptance and distract us from the will of God. We see this from the beginning of time in Genesis in the Garden of Eden with Adam and Eve.

> *Then the Lord God called to the man, "Where are you?" He replied, "I heard you walking in the garden, so I hid. I was afraid because I was naked"* (Genesis 3:9-10 NLT).

Fear is a stronghold the enemy uses against us to keep us isolated. Satan does not want us to be in fellowship with others and tells us constantly that we are not good enough to have relationships with others. My friend, know that God is stronger and more significant than the enemy of this world. He has come to deliver you from your fear and to give you a sound mind, with thoughts on all things relating to the goodness of God. Paul writes in 2 Timothy 1:7, *For God has not given us a spirit of fear, but of power and of love and of a sound mind* (NKJV).

So, you may be wondering, how do we walk through life and not be consumed by fear? That is a great question. We know our thoughts are the most powerful tool to combat our fears—we must know who God is and who we are in Him.

> *And now, dear brothers and sisters, one final thing. Fix your thoughts on what is true, and honorable, and right, and pure, and lovely, and admirable. Think about things that are excellent and worthy of praise* (Philippians 4:8 NLT).

You are unconditionally loved and accepted by our Heavenly Father. As explained in Ephesians 1:6, *to the praise of the glory of His grace, by which He made us accepted in the Beloved* (NKJV).

You belong to Jesus. You are His beloved. It is not necessary to strive or prove yourself. When we understand our acceptance through Christ

Jesus, God fills our hearts and minds with His fullness. Fear can destroy our connection with others, but God's perfect love can heal the hardest hearts.

> *Such love has no fear, because perfect love expels all fear. If we are afraid, it is for fear of punishment, and this shows that we have not fully experienced his perfect love* (1 John 4:18 NLT).

If fear is consuming your life for whatever reason, we urge you to rest in the arms of Jesus and feel His love surrounding you. His love can touch you in the deepest parts of your soul, letting you know you are loved and accepted by the only one who matters. He sees you in your fear.

. . . .

MOLLY WHITEHEAD

Molly Whitehead is from Roxie, Mississippi, and is a graduate of Mississippi State University with a Bachelor's degree in Kinesiology. She aspires to attend graduate school to become an Occupational Therapist.

At Mississippi State, she was a member of the Famous Maroon Band, where she played the clarinet. She currently serves in her church's kids' ministry, showing children the love that Jesus has for them through fun games and recreation. She also loves to sing duets on Sunday mornings with her music minister, Chanse.

Molly has a passion for serving others and shining the light of Christ wherever she goes. She loves sloths, Celsius energy drinks, and the Disney movie "Tangled." In her free time, she enjoys spending time with her friends, listening to music, shopping, and Bible journaling.

Purpose in the Pain

by Molly Whitehead

The senior year of my undergraduate studies at Mississippi State University seemed picture-perfect. I was living my dream of being in the band at MSU and having the best time. I had a great boyfriend who talked more and more about wanting to marry me once we both graduated. I loved my church, my friends, and the entire college atmosphere. Yes, life as a college student was stressful, but I was taking in every moment while it was there.

My faith was a prominent part of my life throughout college. I attended every function at the Baptist Student Union and was there just about every time the doors were open. I went to church on Sunday mornings, Sunday nights for college worship, and midweek Wednesday night services. I was doing everything that your typical Christian college student should be.

I never thought about what would happen if my life were to become something that wasn't picture-perfect. I never imagined what I would do or where I would turn if everything that was once good and comfortable were to crumble before my eyes. But I would soon find out.

For as long as I can remember, my biggest dream has been to be a wife and a mama one day. I wasn't one to go looking for a guy to date, but it bothered me that guys didn't come after me or desire to be with me.

Shortly after I started my freshman year at Copiah-Lincoln Community College, I complained about being single to my roommate so much that she set me up with her boyfriend's roommate. When it finally came time to meet this boy, I was ecstatic that he was even the slightest bit interested in me. He charmed me with his sweet words and his good looks. I was instantly smitten, and we started dating soon after.

I felt loved and cared for in a way I never had before. During that time, I went through all the motions of being a Christian—attending services and small groups at the Baptist Student Union, participating in all the service projects there, and even serving on the lead team during my sophomore year. I did everything that made me look like I had a strong relationship with Christ, everything but spending time and growing in my daily walk with Jesus.

Although I didn't realize it, my relationships with my friends and boyfriend were taking first place in my life; my relationship with Jesus was on the back burner. My walk with Jesus looked good and perfect to others on the outside, but in my heart, I was walking far ahead of Jesus and obliviously making my own plans instead of walking hand in hand with Him and letting Him lead. For the almost three years we were together, my relationship with my boyfriend was my idol. My boyfriend did not know Christ, and although he respected what I believed, he was hindering me in my walk with Christ rather than building it up. I knew this to be true more than anything, but I was held down by the belief that he was one who truly loved me, knew me, and cared for me. I was comfortable where I was in my sin, and I felt as if I was okay with the way my life was.

One September day in the band hall parking lot, the Lord spoke to me almost as if He was sitting in the passenger seat to my right as I listened to worship music in my car. I had just gotten off the phone with my boyfriend after a fight that left us both frustrated with each other. The song *Honey in the Rock* by Brandon Lake played, and with a still small voice, I felt the Lord speaking to my heart saying, "Do you not believe that I can satisfy your soul?" Instead of pushing that voice away like I had so many times before, I listened. This time, He had gotten my attention. I sat in the Lord's presence and just wept there in the driver's seat. I remember vividly almost screaming back at God in my head about how upset and frustrated I was that my plan of being with this boy was just not working out like I had originally planned.

I went to band practice that afternoon, almost in a daze, still wrestling with God in my head and attempting to rationalize why I should continue to stay on this path I had created for myself. After I went home, I spent the entire night on my knees, praying and journaling my frustration, confusion, and anger to God. Although I was experiencing every feeling there was to feel, joy and peace overwhelmed all the others in the presence of the Lord. I had not felt His presence like that in such a long time; it was almost as if I physically felt Jesus wrap His arms around me as I cried on the bedroom floor that night.

That same week, I took a drive with my best friend and told her what the Lord was revealing to me and how I felt I should act on it. Knowing she had been through a similar situation months before, we cried together as I spoke of my fears about the whole situation. Like any good best friend, she encouraged me to obey what the Lord was calling me to do and that she would support me in whatever way she could.

After praying for many days after that, I decided to break off the relationship with my boyfriend. But out of fear, I went back on my decision, and we got back together for a short time in an attempt to mend what was still broken. I kept this to myself and did not tell anyone I had gotten back with him out of fear of what others would think.

When I updated my best friend about what was going on and what I had done, she became frustrated and angry with me for not only keeping it from her but also for not sticking with my decision. Ultimately, this situation caused her to distance herself from me as her friend. I was fighting a war with myself, with God, and now with my best friend. I felt as if no one could see how hard it was for me to make this decision. I felt as if no one understood how confused and lost I felt, and now, not even my best friend was there for me to depend on.

My seemingly picture-perfect and comfortable world was crumbling to pieces, and I did not have any means of being able to fix what was falling apart before me. I was so tired from trying to coordinate my life on my own, but at the same time, I was terrified of the major life changes that were staring me in the face.

As the week went on, I continued to battle within myself, trying to figure out how I was going to fix the situation with my best friend and what I should do about the future regarding my boyfriend. I was truly at a loss. The two people I had depended on for advice, encouragement, and comfort could no longer help me in my current situation. I knew that God loved me and was pursuing me, but I could not understand why everything was all falling apart. In my brokenness and desperation for peace, I stayed in my room at night, listening to worship music and just pouring my heart out to the Lord. Time and time again, He met me right where I was and surrounded me with His loving kindness and peace.

As I sought the Lord in this situation, He kept bringing Hebrews 10:23 to my mind, which has become one of my favorite verses. It says, *Let us hold unswervingly to the hope we profess, for He who promised is faithful* (Hebrews 10:23 NIV). Through this verse, it was almost as if the Lord was repeating the question that He initially asked me in the band hall parking lot: "Do you not believe that I can satisfy your soul?"

I had read and known His promises for us in His Word since I was a child and had experienced His faithfulness in so many ways throughout my life. I had felt His goodness and peace, but I lost sight of that once I thought I had found what my heart truly desired and what would complete me. I came to realize that the desire to be truly known and loved by someone was actually a deep cry within myself to be known and loved by my Creator. I had filled that hole in my heart with love from my boyfriend and friends, but it was insufficient and ultimately left me feeling empty and broken.

After many prayers and tears, I decided to break it off for good with my boyfriend and move forward in mending and growing my relationship with Christ. I also prayed about working things out with my best friend.

After about a week of distancing ourselves from each other, I asked my friend if we could meet up to talk things out. I asked the Lord to guide my words—that I would say things to mend our relationship if His will allowed. I was nervous about the possible outcome of the conversation, but I knew that the Lord was with me.

We met at her apartment. I shared with her my fears about the changes that were to come in my life and that I had never meant to upset or hurt her. She responded with frustration and anger rather than understanding and empathy. I left in tears, feeling misunderstood and unseen in my situation. I could not wrap my mind around why the person who knew me best could no longer see who I was or understand how I was feeling. The Lord had turned my life upside down in just a matter of days.

I drove away listening to worship music. And though I was still confused and sad, I also felt a peace that brought me so much comfort. Again, I felt almost as if the Lord was in the car with me. I cried, prayed, and sang worship music for hours on end, letting the Lord encourage and speak life into my anxious and broken heart through the music and lyrics. I was so confused about why I was losing my best friend in addition to my boyfriend, but I knew the Lord was working in my life. Like the story of the prodigal son, I felt so much peace in returning home after being away for so long.

In the following months, I still struggled with coming to terms with being without my best friend and my boyfriend, but the Lord sustained me each and every day. I took it day by day, and the Lord taught me so many things through that season of my life. He mended my broken heart and met me with abounding grace. He surrounded me with sweet friends from the Baptist Student Union and the girls in my small group who encouraged me, prayed for me, and offered a shoulder to cry on when I needed it. They rallied around me and brought so much comfort in an incredibly challenging season of my life.

I still had days when I wondered why things happened the way they did and why I had to endure so much pain, but I knew the Lord had a plan in the midst of that painful season.

> *Consider it pure joy, my brothers and sisters, whenever you face trials of many kinds, because you know that the testing of your faith produces perseverance. Let perseverance finish its work so that you may be mature and complete, not lacking anything* (James 1:2-4 NIV).

As we all are, I am still a work in progress. I fail the Lord every single day, but He is still shaping me to become more and more like Him each day.

Although I did not see it initially, I now know that the Lord used that pain to allow me to grow closer to Him and become more dependent on Him rather than on other people.

Because of sin, human people in this world—even your closest friends—will often fail you. God will not.

God is the same yesterday, today, tomorrow, and forever. His love for us is unconditional and never-ending, that is, if we choose to receive His love for ourselves.

There is nowhere we can run that is too far for God to meet us. There is no sin too great that He will not forgive. He is the one who satisfies the longing of our souls.

Looking back, I am so overwhelmed by the redeeming grace and love He showed me through that tough season of my life and continues to show me each and every day. The Lord has so many wonderful plans for each person; we just have to trust He knows what is best.

God holds out His hand every day so that we can walk with Him. It is in Him that we have the true hope we can hold onto in difficult times. The Lord does not promise this life will be easy or that there won't be times that challenge our faith, but He does promise to walk with and guide us as His wonderful plan unfolds in each of our lives.

You Are Not Alone in Struggling to Forgive

by Lisa Tofano Hathaway

How do we react when someone hurts us? Does our resentment build? Do we experience feelings of frustration? Or anger? These are some of the many obstacles you may face while trying to forgive someone else—or even yourself. Forgiveness can be difficult, but God's heart is toward forgiveness. God longs for our hearts to be free from the bondage that unforgiveness can cause. Holding on to hurt and pain can steal our time. It can also block our growth toward being all God has called us to be.

Sometimes, pain can be so deep that we cannot fathom forgiveness. When we are hurt, we can have difficulty looking past our emotions and having compassion for the person who hurt us, especially when that person is undeserving of our mercy. But holding onto or refusing to release anger, bitterness, resentment, and unforgiveness can have devastating consequences for our emotional, physical, and spiritual health. It can block us from truly leaning into what God has for us.

Unforgiveness is a sin. And sin harms the sinner most of all. Forgiveness is the key that unlocks the emotional prison that unforgiveness traps us in. Forgiveness is difficult, but it is a process you are never expected to navigate alone. Our gracious Lord holds onto us in our deepest pain. Whatever you have gone through and however you have been hurt, know God has walked with you the whole way. He understands and cares about how you are feeling. That is what is so beautiful about the love of Jesus—He empowers and enables us to be our best selves and reminds us that when we harness His power, He makes forgiveness possible. When we truly understand the depth of God's forgiveness for us, we will trust Him enough to release our power to Him and forgive those who have hurt us. That is why He tells us:

> *But if you refuse to forgive others, your father will not forgive you* (Matthew 6:15 NLT).

Forgiveness is how our relationship with Jesus begins. When we ask Jesus to come into our lives, we ask for His forgiveness for our sins. We recognize our need to be washed clean and made new. In processing that gratitude towards Jesus, we are responsible for and empowered to forgive others.

> *But if we confess our sins to him, he is faithful and just to forgive us our sins and to cleanse us from all wickedness* (1 John 1:9 NLT).

It is difficult to forgive another, especially when they don't apologize or show remorse for their actions. When this obstacle grips you, remember that God forgave us long before we asked for His forgiveness. And further, God chose to act in love and forgiveness even though people rejected him.

> *But God showed his great love for us by sending Christ to die for us while we were still sinners. And since we have been made right in God's sight by the blood of Christ, he will certainly save us from God's condemnation* (Romans 5:8-9 NLT).

When we forgive others, knowing God is close to our hearts through the process, our actions can prove to the other person that we see them more than we see what they did wrong—just as God looks at us.

> *Oh, what joy for those whose disobedience is forgiven, whose sin is put out of sight! Yes, what joy for those whose record the Lord has cleared of guilt, whose lives are lived in complete honesty! When I refused to confess my sin, my body wasted away, and I groaned all day long. Day and night your hand of discipline was heavy on me. My strength evaporated like water in the summer heat. Finally, I confessed all my sins to You and stopped trying to hide my guilt. I said to myself, "I will confess my rebellion to the Lord." And You forgave me! All my guilt is gone.* (Psalm 32:1-5 NLT).

God is with you through the process and challenge of forgiving others. He will empower you to forgive, releasing you from the bondage of unforgiveness. Look to Him because there is no greater example.

MORGAN MOAK

Morgan Moak is from the small town of Brookhaven, Mississippi. She is currently pursuing her studies at Mississippi State University in Kinesiology and will graduate in 2025. She balances her academic pursuits with active involvement in various extracurricular activities, including her membership in the Chi Omega sorority and participation in the Mississippi State Wakeboarding Club. When she's not immersed in her studies or enjoying her hobbies, Morgan can often be found spending quality time with friends cherishing the moments of college.

Beyond her academic and social endeavors, Morgan plans to become an occupational therapist, driven by her innate desire to help others live their lives to the fullest. Her compassionate nature extends beyond her career ambitions; she is deeply devoted to her faith and considers her relationship with the Lord a cornerstone of her life. Whenever the opportunity arises, Morgan eagerly takes the lead in church camps, sharing her personal experiences and faith journey to inspire and uplift others facing similar challenges.

Morgan hopes to spread love, hope, and encouragement through her writing. While writing is a new venture for Morgan, she embraces it with anticipation, eager to witness how the Lord will impact the lives of the readers.

NEVER INVISIBLE TO GOD

by Morgan Moak

Almost everybody has felt unseen at times—that feeling that nobody would care or notice if you were not around.

I have struggled with this feeling more than once; perhaps the most notable time was during my freshman year of college. The whole year was not fun; I was living in misery. On social media, my profile portrayed a happy girl who looked like she had all she could want, including friends, a boyfriend, and a sorority. I think I speak for most when I say social media is just a highlight and a mask. I intentionally used it to make it look like I was thriving at college when, in reality, I was so lonely.

I really do love my life at Mississippi State, but there are days when I feel like I just do not belong. There are times when I have doubted God and been angry with Him, feeling like I was living a life that honored Him, but He did not care. I felt unseen by people at school and even by God.

After finishing high school, I was the most excited person I have ever known to leave my hometown and head to college. I was ready to escape the pain I had endured at the end of high school, which was very rough for me. My close-knit friend group had broken off right before senior year, causing me intense anxiety as some of the girls who had meant the most to me for so many years went their separate ways. As a result, I began having panic attacks, and I felt like all my years of unselfishly loving those people had meant nothing. How could they just walk away after I had been so caring? I just did not understand it. It did not make sense to me why those special friendships did not work out when I thought they would last forever. Needless to say, I was pumped to go to college. I just knew that it was going to be the best thing ever to get out of my small town and meet new people.

But starting college did not go the way I had imagined it would. I had been very involved in high school; I was the soccer captain, a cheerleader, and even a homecoming maid. I was known. Then, suddenly, I had to pick up and leave all the titles behind. And news flash: nobody cared what I had done in high school. When I arrived at college, none of my high school achievements mattered to anybody. In fact, every other girl, it seemed, had the same great resume I did. My first big moment of feeling completely unseen in college was about to happen.

Have you ever felt completely invisible? I have. On bid day.

Bid day is supposed to be a thrilling time when each woman is matched with the sorority that will become her family away from home.

As anticipated, I went into my bid day very excited, but suddenly, I realized nobody there really knew me. The intention was that I would get to spend the next four years with my new best friends, who were also joining the same sorority. However, when I made it to the house, I saw girls in their bid day jerseys who were clearly already friends. I felt utterly alone. Everyone already had their crew. They were all taking group pictures, and nobody saw or cared that I was standing all alone. I sat there at the sorority house, watching everybody around me be so excited to be with their friends and take pictures, and I felt like it just would not matter to a single person if I was there or not. I had never felt that way before, and I hope I never do again.

I was the only one from my hometown who was joining my specific sorority, and it seemed like every other girl there came to college with friends from high school. But not me. I came all alone. I felt like I did not fit in and sat there wondering, *What have I done? Am I really cut out for this?*

I barely said a word that day and for sure cried a few tears, but everyone in my family told me it would get better. They told me I would find my people and would love it. Looking back, I now know I was not the only person who felt that way. Several people felt out of place and a little lost, alone, and unseen. I know the devil was trying to convince me that it was just me, that I was the oddball. I tried to keep my focus on God's plan and continue to live for Him in hopes that friends would come.

I survived bid day, but that was not the only time I felt that way. It often seemed like I was the only one around putting in the effort to talk to people and make friends, so I decided to see if this was true. To test this, I had the not-so-bright idea not to speak to anybody until they spoke to me. Obviously, this was not my best idea. I went to class, to the sorority house for lunch, and then back for dinner, and not a single person spoke to me; therefore, I did not say a word that day. That was the day that I felt the most alone. How could I go all day without a single person saying a word to me? Was I weird?

I would tell myself I used to be so friendly in high school; something must have changed. Maybe COVID ruined my social skills. Maybe I was not cute enough. You name it, and it was going through my head.

My mom told me to try and make an effort, but I felt like I was. I really did feel like I was making an attempt to find friends, but I also did not want to bother people by trying too hard. My extreme fear of rejection caused me to stay to myself. I wanted people to want me again for who I was. I wanted real, genuine friendships with people who loved me.

I was tempted to pretend to be somebody I wasn't so that maybe people would like me just as they had in high school. Yes, it would have been easy to go with the crowd as I had in the past, but all that had gotten me was pain and heartbreak. I chose not to change who I was to fit in, and I am so thankful that I did. Even during this awful time, I stayed true to who I was, which is a child of God. I tried to keep living a life that was honoring to Him, even though I was more than frustrated. I knew the Lord had placed me where I was for many reasons, but mainly so I could do things His way this time, not mine.

However, with these good intentions and thoughts about doing things His way also came fleshly desires to be included. I had to give myself pep talks. I clung to Proverbs 3:5-6, which says, *Trust in the Lord with all your heart, and do not rely on your own understanding; in all your ways acknowledge him, and he will make your paths straight* (ESV). I reminded myself that He would help me find my path, even though I did not see it yet.

Then came spring break, also known as the worst week of my life. Just kidding. That is a little dramatic, but it was a tough week.

I was not really expecting to do anything exciting when the break began, but I soon realized that almost all of my pledge class was headed to the beach. Without me! Nobody told me, and nobody invited me. That really broke me. There are no words to describe how painful that was. I felt invisible. There were actually about five different beach trips, and I did not get invited to go on a single one.

This caused me to ask, "What am I doing wrong?" "How do I make people like me?"

Well, the truth is I was not doing anything wrong, and the girls did not mean any harm. I was just overlooked. But the enemy was in my ear, telling me this meant they did not like me and that something was wrong with me.

My sister, Maley, was at school with me, and I am thankful for her for many reasons, but particularly during that time, as she was the best friend I could ever ask for. She helped me see that the Lord would provide; I just needed to keep pursuing Him. She knew I needed real friends who cared deeply about me and wanted the best for me. I did not want or need surface-level friendships just to get an invitation to an overcrowded beach house. I wanted sisters in Christ who would point me to things of Him.

Maley knew authentic friendships would come for me like they had for her. She helped me see I did not need that particular group of friends that everyone else seemed to be a part of. Instead, I needed a few life partners who would truly love me. She knew these relationships would be worth waiting for. And she knew God was at work, even when I could not see it.

At some point during my freshman year, I quickly realized that throughout high school, I had put my identity in soccer, cheer, and getting every title I could. Those things made me feel known and loved. I did not realize that until I did not have it anymore. But during that first year of college, I felt like I had nothing, so I began to pray and ask God to help me. I would pray for friends, and I would pray to find my place on campus with people who would bring me joy.

Still, when I looked up near the end of the year, it felt like I had gotten almost nowhere. I became angry. I became frustrated. I wondered where God was and why He did not answer my prayers. I felt like I was honoring

Him with my choices, so why would He not give me the friends I wanted so badly?

God helped me see that I had to change my heart. Behind all those prayers, my heart was selfish. I mean, why did I really want friends so badly? Was He not enough? Did I want all of my old friends or moms from my small town to see me doing "great"? The truth is, during that time, I did not think God was enough; I thought I needed more.

While I know for certain the Lord heard my prayers, I also now understand I was asking Him for things that I could claim as my identity. He knew this even if I could not see it. He knew I would take those friendships and put all of my energy into making them perfect; He really needed me to find my peace and identity in Him. The Lord can and will answer prayers, but He always does so in His time.

After my freshman year was over, I put all I had into my relationship with Jesus. He helped me be at peace with who I was in Him instead of who I was on the campus of Mississippi State. I first had to be fully content in Him before He answered my prayers. While it took me being completely broken to see this, He met me in that brokenness and changed my focus to Him and only Him. I am a daughter in Christ before I am a student, sorority girl, sister, or friend.

Not long after I found my contentment in Jesus, He sure enough answered my prayers far beyond what I could have imagined. While I did have peace in who I was in Him, I had a lot of anxiety about returning to a school where I'd felt unseen. I did not want to go back.

At the end of that summer, I was leading at a church camp, and I got placed in a room with a girl my age who attended my school, studied in my major, and was IN MY SORORITY. We had never crossed paths during our freshman year. Her name is Maggy, and our stories were so similar. Freshman year for both of us had been full of just trying to find our place. Once our friendship began to take off, we would talk about how we were so confused about why God did not let us be friends earlier. Why would He allow us both to have such a bad year when we could have been friends all along?

Maggy and I both realized that it was all in His timing. If we had met at a different time and in a different setting, we would not have developed the friendship we did. I was able to return to school with hope and confidence that the Lord did see me and did hear me. It just took me letting go of all my desires and seeing His.

1 Corinthians 10:31 says, *So whether you eat or drink, or whatever you do, do all to the glory of God* (ESV). I know that everything I did in high school and all the things I wanted freshman year were not for the glory of God. They were for the glory of me, my parents, my image, and everybody else. I wanted people to think life for me in college was perfect.

However, once I shifted my focus to God and realized He was all I really needed, He met me where I was and put me at the right place at the right time to meet the perfect people for me.

I am so thankful that God did not answer my prayers when I first prayed them. That sounds weird, I know, but the truth is, any friendships I gained while I was in that mindset would not have been God-honoring. Those friendships probably would have crumbled due to the simple fact that I was not in a place to support others emotionally or spiritually. God knew that.

Find community in God—not in your clubs, organizations, or sorority. Now, I can say that everything I have the privilege to do on my college campus is for the glory of God.

My friendships, involvement, major, and everything else I get the opportunity to be a part of are all centered around bringing the kingdom of Jesus to my campus. My heart has changed, and my focus has changed. The things in my life that bring me joy are not things I have for myself but rather things that honor and glorify the Lord. I strive to be different in everything that I am a part of, and I only hope and pray that Jesus is using me as a vessel and that people see me as a light.

Of course, at times, I still feel lonely, and I still feel unseen—like when I go a week without anybody reaching out to me or when everybody is at one of my "friend's" birthday parties and I am sitting in my bed because I was forgotten once again. I now see those moments as things from the enemy. He wants me to feel unloved. The Lord just wants me to know that I am fully loved.

The truth is that in college, girls are all so busy, and being overlooked sometimes happens. It feels intentional when you are left out, but it rarely is. The more people I reach out to and get to know, the more I learn that they had no idea how they accidentally made me feel.

I am writing this as I begin my junior year. Let me just say it is so fun to watch the Lord's plan unfold right in front of me. Girls now reach out and tell me they've noticed how I live differently, and they want to be my friend. I have gotten the chance to have some awesome conversations that I know are from the Lord. He just keeps pointing me to new girls to talk to and be friends with.

I knew God placed me here for a reason, and it is so fun to find my confidence in Him and fulfill His plan for me. For the first time, I recently walked into the dining room of the sorority house with zero anxiety. I posted on social media out of pure joy—not to keep up an image.

What I don't want you to take away from this is the idea that if you can just make it through freshman year, everything will be great. James 1: 2-4 says, *Count it all joy, my brothers, when you meet trials of various kinds, for you know that the testing of your faith produces steadfastness. And let steadfastness have its full effect, so you may be perfect and complete, lacking in nothing* (ESV). We have to embrace and learn from what we are going through, not just "get through it."

The Lord has given us, is giving us, and will give us trials. These will ultimately mature us. And there is no doubt in my mind that the trial of loneliness matured me beyond what I could ever imagine. There is also no doubt in my mind that the Lord used me in the dark moments. The friendships in high school that did not work out showed me how to love those that hurt me. They also taught me how to seek true friends and led me to the incredible relationships I have now.

My encouragement to you is to continue to persevere through the lonely times and remember that God sees you even when you feel the most unseen. He is working in ways beyond what you can imagine. Our God is not a God of confusion; He will bless you for honoring Him.

Stay true to the Lord. Focus on who He wants you to be, and He will provide.

You Are Not Alone in Your Thoughts

by Lisa Tofano Hathaway and Mendez Nelson

Have you ever thought about what you are thinking about? If not, try it sometime. It can be a challenge. Our minds tend to get off track in seconds. Staying focused on one thing can be challenging. Many of us wrestle with our thoughts. We try to be mindful and present, but it is not easy and seems to take so much effort. Mental patterns and habits are difficult to break. If you have tried this and failed, you are not alone. It is possible to achieve victory in this battle in our minds by becoming aware of our thought patterns and asking for God's help in changing them.

Our minds are incredibly complex. God designed them as part of our souls. He intended us to use them to think about and appreciate Him. Researchers say that our minds are capable of much more than what we use them for in a given day. Typically, we allow our minds to judge, criticize, analyze, evaluate, and condemn ourselves and others. Sadly, we can be so hard on ourselves mentally. We can actually use our minds to be mean and cruel to ourselves. Our minds can beat us up; this is incredibly exhausting. The Bible commands us to love our neighbors as we love ourselves, but if we are tearing ourselves down inside our own minds, then we are not loving ourselves well at all. The Bible says we have the mind of Christ. His thoughts are kind, gentle, patient, loving, and tender. We can choose to put the truths of the Word of God into our minds so we can think about ourselves the way He thinks of us.

It is not easy to stop unhealthy thought patterns we have developed in our minds, but with God's help, all things are possible. It seems easier to let our minds shift into neutral. Activities like scrolling through social media, playing computer games, or binge-watching a TV series can help us avoid thinking about what we are thinking about. Some of us even choose to numb out with alcohol or other substances. However, none of these strategies are effective against negative thoughts.

To become truly victorious in our thoughts and win the battle being waged in our minds, we must go to the Source. Our Creator has a great deal to say about how our minds work and how they should be used.

Paul, in Philippians 4:8, encourages us, *whatever is true, whatever is noble, whatever is right, whatever is pure, whatever is lovely, whatever is admirable—if anything is excellent or praiseworthy—think about such things* (NIV).

In 2 Corinthians 10:5, Paul explains what we are to do with our thinking. He states, *We demolish arguments and every pretension that sets itself up against the knowledge of God, and we take captive every thought to make it obedient to Christ* (NIV).

Brothers and sisters, stop thinking like children. In regard to evil be infants, but in our thinking be adults (1 Corinthians 14:20 NIV).

Additionally, the Bible mentions the benefits of meditating on Scripture. The New Oxford American Dictionary says that to meditate means to think deeply or focus one's mind for a period of time in silence for religious or spiritual purposes. Joshua 1:8 states, *Keep this Book of the Law always on your lips; meditate on it day and night, so that you may be careful to do everything written in it. Then you will be prosperous and successful* (NIV). Does this mean we are to superglue Bibles to our lips and stay awake all night thinking deeply about what it says? Absolutely not! But it does mean we are to speak and think and act in a way that honors God.

Spending time in His Word, reflecting on what it says, and memorizing verses feeds our spirits and makes us grow strong spiritually. Meditating and memorizing God's Word benefits our minds greatly. The Word of God actually renews our minds. Freedom exists for our minds. We can begin today to win the battle in our minds by becoming aware of what we are thinking about, filling our minds with Scripture, and asking for God's help. Our mental health is worth it.

God sees your desire to be free. He is there with you and will help you every step of the way. You are never alone in your thoughts.

. . . .

ALEXIS BERRYHILL

Alexis Berryhill loves the Lord and serving in ministry. She is energized by sharing God's love through music.

Since yielding to the Lord's call for her life, Alexis has immersed herself in her church choir and praise team and serves as the pianist.

Dedicated to sharpening her craft, Alexis is pursuing a Bachelor's in Music and Worship from Lee University. She is part of a ministering travel choir and band, the Ladies of Lee and Hilltop Worship. She enjoys traveling with these two groups to minister to people of all different walks of life through music and the power of worship.

Alexis is an avid traveler and is always up for an adventure. Among her favorite travels was her trip to Israel in 2023. "This trip completely changed my life and opened my eyes to the spiritual poverty of people across the globe." She lives with the passion to travel near and abroad to share the Gospel and freedom Jesus brings.

Alexis enjoys deep conversations, singing, and hiking with her friends.

The Lord revealed to her years ago that she would be a writer, so this chapter is a promise come true! He is faithful!

Diamonds in the Rough

by Alexis Berryhill

What do you do when your life suddenly goes completely out of control? When you are in an endless cycle you never thought you would have to experience? When you feel like you are being pulled farther and farther out in a riptide where the waves are gushing over your face and you cannot breathe? Can you relate? I have been there, and I see you.

The only way for a diamond to form is through crushing and refining. Likewise, the most traumatizing and faith-shaking experiences of our lives bring about the most beautiful testimonies. Through the crushing, Jesus is making you into a beautiful diamond.

This is my story of how fire forged me into a diamond.

Tears begin to roll down my cheeks as my mom explains to me she is leaving. I am six years old; my brother, Luke, is only four. I cannot comprehend how a mom can leave her children, much less the love of her life. I sob while begging my parents to apologize to one another. Divorce is a word I have never heard before. *What does this mean? Will we ever get to see our momma again?* My broken, six-year-old heart could never understand what the following years would look like, and if someone had told me the emotional trauma I would have to work through, I do not know if I would have been up for the challenge.

As my brother and I moved in with our dad, we finally began to experience normalcy and stability. We attempted to visit our mom on several occasions, but she always explained she was busy. Prior to their divorce, Daddy had to rescue my brother and me out of drug dealers' homes, rush to car wrecks because our mom was high on drugs, and intervene in many other traumatizing experiences. Momma struggled very intensely with drug addiction and men. I could never understand why I was never enough for her. My daddy has always been a good man who prioritized mine and my brother's safety, even at the loss of his own.

In the midst of this heartbreak, God somehow seems to always work things for good.

When I turned eight years old, my dad reunited with a lady he knew from the church he went to as a teenager. She immediately asked, "Where are you going to church?" At the time, we were not going anywhere. She willfully and excitedly told us of a church we needed to begin attending. The next Sunday, my dad took Luke and me to church.

Suddenly everything changed for us in a way I could have never imagined.

We began to get involved in multiple ways, including the church's drama team rehearsals, children's church, plays, and choir rehearsals. This was the church where my brother and I gave our hearts to the Lord. The church was an hour away, but we knew this was where the Lord wanted us to go. We felt so loved by everyone there, and they became family. By that point, we had lost contact with our mom, but our dad did an amazing job taking on the roles of both parents—he painted my nails, brushed my hair, played outside with Luke and me, and provided everything else that would give us a good childhood. Thankfully, we lived right next to my dad's parents, so they helped raise us as well. As we all know, it's every kid's dream to live next to their grandparents.

Even greater things began to unfold. After I turned twelve, my dad married Caroline, the children's pastor at our church. We were able to move closer to the church and begin a new life. With the start of a new season, we also had a new school to attend. Since Caroline was a high school teacher, we quickly found our place. I was involved in several academic and extracurricular activities, including band. In the afternoons, I was the "cool" kid who got to hang out at the high school before it was time to go home. I had many friends, made good grades, and was very content with where I was. God strategically placed people in my path that loved me like family, even when my own was incomplete.

In my 9th grade year, I auditioned for color guard and made the team. Never in my wildest dreams could I have prepared for what happened next. One Friday night, I was marching into another school's football stadium and saw a face no child could ever forget. It was my mother. After years of being estranged from her, she was suddenly back in my life. I was taken aback by her cold, empty eyes. *Where was the mom I once knew?* She was buried deep under years of addiction and hurt—trying to find peace in all the wrong places. My heart dropped, and all I could think was, *How did she find me? What should I do?* I felt overwhelmingly alone. My hands were clammy; I felt frozen in time. I did not know what was about to unfold. After all, a fourteen-year-old is never prepared to face the tension of her mother alone. I am far from a confrontational person, so the last thing I wanted was a big scene. The night went on, and I avoided my mom the entire game. When the game was over, it was such a relief as the band bus pulled away from the piece of my life I wanted to disappear. How could my life continue normally after this?

My mom appeared at my next two games. I felt waves of panic rush over me. By the last game, I knew I had to do something. I avoided my mom the whole game, and it broke my heart to see her cry because of my decision to stay away. I knew I couldn't let my mom be involved in my life. I knew there was so much darkness in her it would only negatively impact me. When I got home, I spoke with my dad and decided I should message my mom to tell her I did not want to see her anymore. It was an extremely difficult thing for me to have to tell my own mother, but I had to protect myself—spiritually, physically, mentally, and emotionally.

After disconnecting from my mother, life returned to normal—or as normal as it could get. My deep love for Jesus inspired many people; however, some saw it as an opportunity for ridicule. I passionately wanted people to experience the same love of Jesus I had experienced—one that only comes from Him. After a couple of months of standing firm, I began to go home and cry myself to sleep. The once-confident girl started to be ruled by insecurity and loneliness. I began to believe lies like I would never be enough, I could never live up to what God called me to be, and I was not beautiful. I felt like I was falling down a slippery slope of negative self-image, and it was impossible to gain my footing.

In May, I got the news no one wants to hear: my mom had passed away from a heroin overdose. I had been struggling before, but this led me to fall into a deeper, darker pit of hopelessness. I felt numb, yet I felt all things at the same time— things like hurt, anger, anxiety, and depression. Thoughts began to intrude my mind. *What if I could have done something? Is it my fault? Is it because I told her I didn't want to see her anymore?* The walls began to close around me. *When did I stop being enough?* Over the next couple of months, I continued to cry myself to sleep, all while burying my true feelings from the people closest to me.

The next football season came, and I earned the privilege of leading my high school band as the drum major. I loved every moment of leading but had intense inward struggles I could no longer contain. The pressure I put on myself began to rise, and I began to fall apart from the inside out. There was not a day that went by when I did not have several panic attacks—even during football games. My teachers began to notice and worry. I attempted relentlessly to suppress my emotions to appear strong for everyone else, but I felt truly hopeless inside. My parents noticed I was not doing well, so I went to the doctor. The doctor prescribed anxiety medication, but it never took the deep void away that was inside me, so I stopped taking the medicine. I felt thousands of miles away from the girl who defended the gospel to her friends. Somewhere in this process, I completely lost all sight of who I was in Christ.

Months went by, and I began to self-harm. I hated looking in the mirror and could not possibly see myself as the role model other people saw me as. I was a whitewashed tomb—clean on the outside but full of dirt on the inside. I felt like I was screaming and no one could hear or understand. I became the girl in the church pew who appeared to be fine but deep down, was hurting more than she could ever put into words. I thought, *Who would believe me? They may think I'm just trying to get attention.*

After arriving home one night, I became so depressed that I lost all desire to do anything. I wanted to disappear. Laying in the darkness of my room was somehow comforting, yet I felt as though I was drowning. My pastor's wife called and prayed for me, but there was such a cloudiness I could not see through.

One Wednesday night at church, a guest speaker from Africa came to lead our service. During the altar call, she walked straight to me, hugged me, and, somehow, supernaturally saw the depression and anxiety that was trying to take control of my life. As she hugged me, she spoke encouraging words and blessings over my life. I realized then that the Lord sent someone across the world just to minister to me. Since I had attended youth camp as a little kid, I knew that God was calling me into worship ministry, and I suddenly began to realize that Satan's one goal for my life was to kill, steal, and destroy all that God created me to be. But God was in control, and He gave me a little glimpse of sunshine again that night. However, my battle was not over yet.

After another month of continued struggle against this stronghold in my life, my dad had a difficult conversation with me. All those months, I desperately strived to appear unbothered to my family and everyone else, but now, all those barriers were gone. My dad and I talked about everything, including the emotions, self-harm, and panic attacks. He helped me realize the Lord actually DOES care about me—and that He coordinated everything in my life so lovingly and meticulously to bring about a plan and purpose for my good and His glory.

If it was not for God's love, grace, and mercy, I could have ended up just like my mother—lost, broken, or even dead. The Lord proved His faithfulness in every area of my life and instantly gave me unspeakable joy. He enabled me to forgive every hurt my mom caused. I recommitted to my pursuit of God and the ministry He called me to with every fiber of my being.

At the close of a more recent year, I prayed and asked God to give me one word I could expound upon in the upcoming year—a word I could apply to every area of my life. One that would cause me to grow closer to Him in every way. He began to confirm this single word to me through songs and scriptures on numerous different occasions.

Abide.

> *Abide in Me, and I in you. As the branch cannot bear fruit of itself, unless it abides in the vine, neither can you, unless you abide in Me* (John 15:4 NKJV).

According to Strong's Concordance, the Greek word used for "abide" in this scripture is "meño," which means "to stay, remain, wait." [1]

I realized that God was bringing me back to the basics. Just as a tree cannot grow without a root system, I cannot grow without being rooted in God. And if the tree does not grow, it will not produce fruit. For me, being rooted in God consists of sitting at His feet daily to learn from Him, reading and studying His Word, worshiping, praying, and heeding His voice. Your routine may look different than mine, but the goal is to lean into Him, abide in Him, and get as close to Jesus as you are humanly able. When we do this, we will produce good fruit that will become a magnet God uses to draw others to Him. Once we begin to know God intimately, we will start to believe His words at the very core of our being.

Abiding in Jesus is not always easy. In fact, it is a constant, daily battle between the flesh and the spirit. The flesh constantly wars against the spirit because Satan does not want us to walk in the victory Jesus gave His life for us to have. The devil would love nothing more than to trap you in feelings of isolation, fear, depression, anxiety, and other negative mindsets. As in my story, his sole purpose is to kill, steal, and destroy you. The devil shows no mercy—he never slacks on trying to destroy us, and he will never stop until we depart from this earth and enter our eternal home. As you are just beginning your life out of high school, going to college, or joining the workforce, you need to know that life will not always be like this momentary struggle. Transition amidst trying to learn who you are, what you want to do, and what people you choose to let in your life is difficult. Satan will come at you with lies such as: "You will never be good enough," "Who do you think you are to believe you can actually achieve your dreams?" "God is mad at you," and sometimes the worst of all, "You have to do this alone."

I am going to stop you right here.

You are never alone! Even if you do not have people to stand by your side, the King of the entire universe is on your side. Romans 8:31 says, *What then shall we say to these things? If God is for us, who can be against us?* (NKJV)

So, how can we combat these daunting lies the enemy throws at us? The only way you can combat a lie is with the truth. And truth is found in God's Word. He is the only one who is able to define us—the Creator gets to define His creation. People are not in charge of creating you. The devil is not in charge of creating you. *God Himself* created you. If you begin to feel the opposite of what your Creator says about you, speak the scriptures aloud and rebuke the enemy in Jesus' name. You cannot stand idly by and allow the enemy to win. Here are some scriptures you can use to deter these negative thoughts:

> *Yet in all these things we are more than conquerors through Him who loved us* (Romans 8:37 NKJV).

> *But God demonstrates His own love toward us, in that while we were still sinners, Christ died for us* (Romans 5:8 NKJV).

For You formed my inward parts; You covered me in my mother's womb. I will praise You, for I am fearfully and wonderfully made; Marvelous are Your works, And that my soul knows very well (Psalm 139:13-14 NKJV).

For though we walk in the flesh, we do not war according to the flesh. For the weapons of our warfare are not carnal but mighty in God for pulling down strongholds, casting down arguments and every high thing that exalts itself against the knowledge of God, bringing every thought into captivity to the obedience of Christ, and being ready to punish all disobedience when your obedience is fulfilled (2 Corinthians 10:3-6 NKJV).

> *Be anxious for nothing, but in everything by prayer and supplication, with thanksgiving, let your requests be made known to God; and the peace of God, which surpasses all understanding, will guard your hearts and minds through Christ Jesus. Finally, brethren, whatever things are true, whatever things are noble, whatever things are just, whatever things are pure, whatever things are lovely, whatever things are of good report, if there is any virtue and if there is anything praiseworthy—meditate on these things. The things which you learned and received and heard and saw in me, these do, and the God of peace will be with you* (Philippians 4:6-9 NKJV).

These are just a few scriptures I apply to my life when my thoughts go rampant. As you read and study the Bible, you will discover that God's Word is living and active, sharper than a double-edged sword. You can find an answer to any situation you face in God's Word. That alone is where your freedom is found—not in people or situations. These things are wavering. Your life *must* be built upon the firm foundation: God Himself. As you focus on Him, your circumstances will grow dim and no longer dictate the power of your Father.

Friend, I see you. I understand your hurt, your feelings of entrapment, and your tears. This season will not last forever.

He who calls you is faithful.

You will soon become a beautiful diamond.

[1] Greek concordance: μείνατε (meinate)—5 occurrences. Accessed February 29, 2024. https://biblehub.com/greek/meinate_3306.htm.

YOU ARE NOT ALONE IN MENTAL STRUGGLES

by Mendez Nelson

Every thought that pops into our minds does not originate with us. Our enemy, the devil, uses our minds as a battleground. He sends wrong thoughts to attack us; however, we have control over whether we allow these thoughts to enter and stay or banish them. The Bible calls Jesus the truth and the devil a liar. Jesus Himself declared in John 14:6, "I am the way and the truth and the life. No one comes to the Father except through me" (NIV). In contrast, Jesus describes Satan as *"...a murderer from the beginning, not holding to the truth, for there is no truth in him. When he lies, he speaks his native language, for he is a liar and the father of lies"* (John 8:44b NIV). We must choose who we will believe and what we allow our minds to be filled with—the truth or the lies.

> *We demolish arguments and every pretension that sets itself up against the knowledge of God, and we take captive every thought to make it obedient to Christ* (2 Corinthians 10:5 NIV).

God knew the intense mental battle we would face during our lives on earth, so He provided us weapons to fight this war. Ephesians 6:10-18 gives a detailed description of the armor God designed for our protection. One of the pieces of that armor is referred to as the helmet of salvation, which is used to shield our minds. For though we live in the world, we do not wage war as the world does. The weapons we fight with are not the weapons of the world. On the contrary, they have divine power to demolish strongholds (2 Corinthians 10:3-4 NIV).

God blessed us with the ability to control what we think. Through Christ, we have power over our own minds. *For God hath not given us the spirit of fear; but of power, and of love, and of a sound mind* (2 Timothy 1:7 KJV). As believers, God actually places His mind inside of us. *But we have the mind of Christ* (1 Corinthians 2:16b NIV).

Because God gave us free will to choose, He does not force us to think a certain way; however, He provides us with guidelines for living His way, teaching us through Paul's words: *Do not conform to the pattern of this world, but be transformed by the renewing of your mind* (Romans 12:2a NIV). God renews our minds when we choose to read and live by God's truths. In Philippians 4, Paul even gives us a list of things to think about so we can have peace instead of anxiety. That list says we should think about things that are true, noble, right, pure, lovely, admirable, excellent, and praiseworthy. Although our fallible human minds are sure to drift off course, we can choose to shift our thoughts back onto the right path.

Set your minds on things above, not on earthly things (Colossians 3:2 NIV).

You will keep in perfect peace those whose minds are steadfast, because they trust in you (Isaiah 26:3 NIV).

For no matter how many promises God has made, they are "Yes" in Christ. And so through him the "Amen" is spoken by us to the glory of God. Now it is God who makes both us and you stand firm in Christ. He anointed us, set his seal of ownership on us, and put his Spirit in our hearts as a deposit, guaranteeing what is to come (2 Corinthians 1:20-22 NIV).

When we choose to believe and receive God's promises, we will become victorious in learning to keep our thoughts focused on the Lord. *"For my thoughts are not your thoughts, neither are your ways my ways," declares the Lord. "As the heavens are higher than the earth, so are my ways higher than your ways and my thoughts than your thoughts"* (Isaiah 55:8-9 NIV).

If you feel your mind straying or being filled with thoughts that are not from God, ask God to help you. He already knows what you are thinking anyway. *You perceive my thoughts from afar* (Psalm 139:2b NIV).

Together, let's make it a practice to pray the same prayer King David prayed in Psalm 139:23-24: *Search me, God, and know my heart; test me and know my anxious thoughts. See if there is any offensive way in me, and lead me in the way everlasting* (NIV).

Amen!

. . . .

SARAH DELAFOSSE

Sarah DeLafosse is a Senior Communications major at Texas A&M University who will graduate in the fall of 2024. She hopes to attend law school or pursue a long-term career at H-E-B corporate.

Sarah grew up in Cypress, Texas, with her mom, dad, younger sister Kate, and their dog Sadie. She was active in her home church and enrolled in online, dual credit, and co-op classes throughout high school.

As an Enneagram 3w2, Sarah is goal-oriented and determined. After attending Blinn College in Bryan for a year, she transferred to Texas A&M in the fall of 2023. There, she is involved in a variety of organizations. She was a member of a sorority, has been a fish camp counselor twice, and is an active member of a half-social, half-service organization focused on serving and giving back to Brazo County.

Sarah loves being surrounded by friends and family, being outdoors, watching movies, thrifting, and baking. While the road to where she is today hasn't been linear, Sarah feels very blessed to live the life she does. In times of uncertainty, some of her favorite Bible verses are Psalm 121:1 and Romans 12:9.

LIFT YOUR EYES TO THE LORD

by Sarah DeLafosse

Even though we walk in God's divine plan, that does not mean our lives will be without hardship and struggle. That has been one of the hardest pills I have had to swallow as a Christian.

Before I dive into my story, I should tell you that I sometimes forget how good God is. The truth is that He is good all the time, but sometimes, I get so caught up in my world that I forget to lift my eyes and see what He has for me. I forget or doubt His plans for me, and instead of letting Him drive the car of my life, I try to take the wheel.

> *I lift my eyes to the mountains— where does my help come from? My help comes from the Lord, the Maker of heaven and earth. He will not let your foot slip— he who watches over you will not slumber; indeed, he who watches over Israel will neither slumber nor sleep* (Psalm 121:1-4 NIV).

Howdy, my name is Sarah DeLafosse. I am a junior communications major at Texas A&M University from Cypress, Texas. When I was in high school, I thought there was a very specific mold for how college would go for me. The world preached that the college experience is the best years of your life—the time when you meet tons of great people and constantly have a blast. When I got to school and this expectation did not hold true, I was disappointed and felt alone. It didn't help much knowing my disappointment partially occurred because I took a different path than everyone else I knew and allowed comparison and jealousy to take root in my life.

Let's flashback to my senior year of high school. I struggled with mental health around the time college applications were due. I did not see how I would be ready to go to college and live on my own. I felt extremely dependent on my parents, and, at one point, I was seeing both my therapist and psychiatrist several times a month. I was not motivated to apply to colleges because I found it difficult to see a future at any of them. I found it difficult to see any future at all.

I did begin an application for Texas A&M. Olivia, one of my best childhood friends whom I had known since I was two years old, and I planned to live together in the dorm on campus. However, I failed to submit my grades, which led to a rejection letter in the spring. Simultaneously, I was struggling with simple tasks like brushing my teeth and was diagnosed with Dysthymia and placed on anti-depressants to help with my depression and anxiety. I was content to stay at home and take more community college classes. The Lord shows Himself to each person differently. He knows I need visual and clear signs of His plan for me because, as I said, even though I am working on it, I often forget the extent of His goodness and grace.

For about a week or so after my rejection, my mom and I brainstormed every possible option for my immediate future. We made pro and con lists and assessed costs. Then, Olivia's mom reached out to my mom, suggesting I attend Blinn, a junior college in College Station, Texas, which serves as a feeder school to Texas A&M. She said that if I did, Olivia and I could still live together in an apartment, and I could get college credit for a lower price and then transfer to TAMU.

After further investigating and praying about my options, my mom and I decided Blinn would be a great opportunity for me. I could still live with Olivia, and the school was not too far, so I could easily drive home if I needed my family.

After making the decision, God clearly blessed my path, giving me a very clear sign that I was walking in His will. Olivia and I ended up living in a sketchy off-campus apartment complex with two random roommates—as this was our only option. We had moved into the apartment with minimal communication with these girls and had zero clue about their character or if they would be even half-decent roommates. We assumed, based on the minimal information we knew about them, that we would not get along. That and the fact that, for most people, being paired with random roommates ends horribly. However, Kensley and Kayla became two of my biggest blessings during my freshmen year.

The hardest part of my first year of college was watching everyone I knew who went to A&M get plugged into organizations and meet new people. Back home, many of my favorite people were those I worked with, so I assumed that transferring and working at a different franchise would be beneficial. However, the new franchise wanted to cut my pay but keep me on for my expertise. So, I ended up quitting and lost that outlet. I began to feel lonely. It seemed there were very few options for me to meet new people. Every day, I went to my classes and sat next to strangers who did not know me or care to know me—or at least that's what it felt like. While everyone else seemed to be getting accepted into new organizations, I felt excluded. And there were moments when hurtful things were said about me not being able to understand how things worked at A&M because I attended Blinn.

It was hard to accept that people I was once close with were moving on and making new friends. I no longer got invitations to activities, and it was hard not to take it personally. It was hard to believe that I was a person worth knowing. I was frustrated with God. *Why would He lead me down a path filled with more loneliness? Weren't these supposed to be the best years of my life?*

Transferring to a new job did not work. Every student organization I tried to join seemed like a dead end. And it felt like every day that passed, my friends I came to college with reached out to me less and less often. There were many moments when I doubted the decision I had made, thinking I'd have been better off staying at home.

Whether it was my personal stigma or the opinions of people around me, I began to feel like I was "less than" because I attended Blinn. I felt like I had to prove I was intelligent. Every time someone asked where I went to school, I overexplained my situation, compelled to give the entire rundown of my situation—that my mental health wasn't the greatest and that Blinn was better for me financially. I would talk myself in circles, trying to prove that I could've gotten into A&M if it hadn't been for extenuating circumstances. I cared how people perceived me; I was searching for my worth in validation from people in my life instead of through God.

I have always struggled with truly being myself. But during this time in my life, I began realizing I do not need to fit any mold or box that someone wants me to fit in.

It is so beautiful how God works. Despite the fact I was growing, it was still hard to shake the feeling of worthlessness when certain friends stopped texting and reaching out. But God knew, far in advance, that I would have these struggles, and He knew that I would need people in my life that I simply could not escape. Kensley, Kayla, and Olivia were exactly those people. They were my friends even when I found it hard to make friends. No one made me laugh harder than these three; the vibes were unparalleled in apartment 3308. Kayla taught me so many life lessons—she taught me tips and tricks in the kitchen and advised me on how to transfer from Blinn to A&M, as she had done so herself the year before. Kensley and I were so similar—like we lived parallel lives in different cities. It is hard to remember my life before meeting her. She is still one of my best friends and is one of the most tenacious and loyal people I know; my college experience would be abysmal without her. And, of course, Olivia. Olivia has shown me how to love people best and made me a better person in the last three years I've lived with her. She is my family here in College Station. My life is so much better because she is in it.

As apartment mates, we made lists of things we could all do together; we played bingo, saw Christmas lights, went to football games, cooked together, collected aluminum cans for money, binge-watched *Survivor,* and enjoyed every moment we had together.

What is so divine about all this is that if I had submitted my grades to Texas A&M University, I would have never met Kensley and Kayla; there would have been no overlap in our lives. That is how I know God has a hand in my life. These roommates brought me so much joy at a time when I could've been completely alone. There is no doubt in my mind they were placed in my life by God. If it were not for my struggles with Dysthymia during my senior year, I would've submitted my grades to A&M, I would've gotten in, and Olivia and I would have lived on campus in a dorm, having never crossed paths with Kensley or Kayla.

Another blessing God gave me during this time was my boyfriend. Zack and I had worked together back home, and we started dating when I got to college. At the time, I felt like not many people understood my situation.

Even if they understood where I went to school, they did not understand what it felt like to live in my shoes. Zack understood. Even though we were an hour away from each other, he understood what it was like to go to a community college and then transfer to a four-year institution. Amongst all his great qualities and reasons why I love him, Zack is a great listener, is goofy, makes me laugh so hard I snort, allows me to be the most unfiltered version of myself, and is compassionate. I am consistently baffled by how much he knows. To top it all, he is a friend to all. I am so extremely blessed God placed him in my life. In moments when I felt unloved and unseen, God used Zack to build me up. It is a privilege for me to be loved by and to love Zack, Olivia, Kensley, and Kayla. The strategic placement of people in my life during a time of loneliness cannot be explained by anything else except God.

When I lift my eyes to the Lord, He shows me there is absolutely no reason to doubt His presence in my life. Yet I still doubt, and He still shows up.

When I think back to my freshman year, at the time it was hard to see all these blessings. It was difficult to shake my feelings of unworthiness. I know this may sound discouraging, but it took me until junior year to really find my place.

If you are going through something difficult, do not be discouraged. Keep trying. It is all too easy to walk through life with your head down, but I want to encourage you to consciously lift your eyes to God. When you do, He will show you His goodness.

There was a moment during my sophomore year when I was walking through campus in the rain. I hate the rain. Something about it has always scared me—I hate driving in it, and I hate using umbrellas because, for some reason, I feel like it is embarrassing to use my umbrella. LOL. On that day, it was pouring. I was already running late for class and could not find my rain jacket or umbrella. So I walked thirty minutes in the rain wearing a sopping wet sweatshirt and sweatpants. I showed up five minutes late for the class, which happened to be one where there was a quiz every week. By the time I arrived, the class had already taken the quiz. Water was visibly dripping from my clothing as I sat through an hour and fifteen-minute course. After, I asked the professor if I could take the quiz. He said no. Soaking wet, I walked out of class, trying not to cry.

I remember that day vividly for this reason: I walked out of class feeling defeated, but when I lifted my eyes, God showed me He was there. With my head down, watching my pants swish between my legs as water dripped off them, I heard my name. I looked up to see a girl I barely knew from my sorority. She saw I was drenched and offered to give me her umbrella at the risk of her becoming drenched, just like me. That moment has stuck with me because, although I felt completely alone, when I lifted my eyes, God placed someone I knew right in front of me. This friend normally did not have class on that side of campus, and we had never crossed paths on campus before. By lifting my eyes at a moment when I felt unseen, I was seen.

A word of warning to any incoming freshmen or transfer student: it can be hard. It can be hard to find your place, especially when it feels like everyone else has already found theirs. I promise you they have not.

You are someone worth knowing!

When I feel like God is not there, I cling to Psalm 121:1-4 (NIV): *I lift my eyes to the mountains— where does my help come from? My help comes from the Lord, the Maker of heaven and earth. He will not let your foot slip— he who watches over you will not slumber; indeed, he who watches over Israel will neither slumber nor sleep. This passage is important to me and my story. In moments when I doubt God and His goodness, the second I lift my eyes, the*

Lord provides me a tangible sign that God, who watches over ME, will neither slumber nor sleep. This holds true for you, too. The God who watches over YOU does not slumber nor sleep.

There will be moments when you will question His plan because it is not always easy. I wish I could tell you I never feel alone today or that I do not struggle with anxiety or depression anymore. I do still struggle with those things, but I hold on to those moments when God has shown Himself to me, and I hold out for the moments when He will do so again.

Through different student organizations He has placed in my life, God has used other people to show me I am worth knowing. I believe He will do the same for you. As you read this, it may seem as if I had all these beautiful moments with God overnight, but it took me two years to be fully content with being myself. Two years to fully believe that I am someone worth knowing.

It feels like a cliché, but comparison is indeed the thief of joy. Do not compare yourself to other people. What may work for them might not work for you! We are all on a different path, working towards different goals.

Your circle does not have to be extensive—having quality friends who will stick by you is far more valuable than knowing many people only on a surface level. It is so easy to get wrapped up in the who-knows-who game. It is challenging not to feel isolated when people start talking about all the people that make them connected to each other. But always know you are not alone.

You are seen by Him.

You are worth knowing.

In the moments it feels like you are unseen, lift your eyes to the Lord.

You Are Not Alone
in Your Anger

by Lisa Tofano Hathaway

Anger is a powerful weapon the enemy will use against us in many situations. It can lead to sin and resentment, and it can rob you of the blessings God has for you. Satan wants anger to ruminate in our minds—this gives him the opportunity to tempt and lead us to sin against someone else, perhaps even God. But you are not alone. Anger is an emotion that God understands and knows we will have. Anger itself is not a sin, but when you feel it creep or even storm in, be careful, for what we do as a result of anger may be sinful.

> *"Don't sin by letting anger control you." Don't let the sun go down while you are still angry, for anger gives a foothold to the devil* (Ephesians 4:26-27 NLT).

Anger can fester inside of us and, if not handled right, spur us on to actions that cause harm to others. Perhaps the greatest danger of retaliating against others in our anger is the risk of isolating someone and even causing them to stray away from the faith because of our actions. Therefore, we should be slow to become angry, filtering all our emotions through God and asking Him how He wants us to respond.

Anger can be a natural emotion when we go through trials and suffering. But God wants and empowers us to have the qualities of righteousness to face our trials, showing the world that, with God, there is a better way to handle our negative emotions. He is always available to help us rightly discern our response.

> *Understand this, my beloved brothers and sisters. Let everyone be quick to hear [be a careful, thoughtful listener], slow to speak [a speaker of carefully chosen words and], slow to anger [patient, reflective, forgiving]; for the [resentful, deep-seated] anger of man does not produce the righteousness of God [that standard of behavior which He requires from us]* (James 1:19-20 AMP).

As creations of God, we are to do all things to glorify Him. When we allow our emotions of anger to take over, we can lose sight of what is right and the One who gives us life. It can be difficult to overlook what someone has done to us or how some circumstance has impacted us and made us angry, but if we allow that anger to swell up, become rage, and control us, we will miss out on the bigger picture of what God can do in those moments. He may miraculously calm the storm or, even more miraculously, give His peace during the raging storm. Don't miss out on the blessings God has prepared by stubbornly handling things your own way.

> *The discretion of a man makes him slow to anger, and his glory is to overlook a transgression* (Proverbs 19:11 NKJV).

God gives us an extraordinary example of how we should react when angry. We all do things that should infuriate God, but He is slow to anger and repeatedly shows us His grace when we mess up—even when it doesn't seem to make sense to us. Likewise, there may be times when we feel like it does not make sense for us not to retaliate or blow up, but we must let it go and look to God. His Word shows us over and over how He offers grace and mercy despite our actions. God does get angry, but the Bible makes it clear that His grace and mercy far exceed His wrath. God loves and protects us as His children, and we are called to reflect His image. That means we are to love and protect others as well.

> *The Lord is merciful and gracious, Slow to anger, and abounding in mercy* (Psalm 103:8 NKJV).

> *Refrain from anger and turn from wrath; do not fret—it leads only to evil. For those who are evil will be destroyed, but those who hope in the Lord will inherit the land* (Psalm 37:8-9 NIV).

God is with you when you are angry. Do not be afraid to acknowledge your anger and emotions and go to Him for guidance for your response. Be still. Rest in His presence. Breathe Him in. He sees you.

. . . .

PARIS VANCE

Paris Vance grew up in church but has faithfully loved the Lord since the summer of 2021, when God changed her life. As a counselor at a Christian summer camp, everything changed for her.

Since then, Paris has graduated from Mississippi State University with a Bachelor's in Interior Design and married the boy she met working at summer camp. Her husband, Ryan, and their furry baby named Oakley now live in Dallas, Texas, where they met!

Paris believes in the power of life change and prayer. She loves leading small groups and pouring into those around her. She believes that God can use any story and make it His.

She enjoys all things creative, traveling, and has always loved writing. This chapter is her first published opportunity to share her story!

YOUR SMALL YES

by Paris Vance

For many months leading up to May 2021, I was full of dread and disbelief that I would actually be a camp counselor for Sky Ranch Camps.

I had gotten tricked into interviewing to work at the Christian summer camp, which was all fun and games until I had to buy the long khaki shorts and realized I was scared of children. How in the world was I going to share the gospel with kids when I hadn't opened my Bible or even gone to church in months? I felt severely unqualified and out of place. I kept thinking, *They've got the wrong person. If they only knew...*

I finally made it to camp and met the kindest people whose joy radiated from them. They were welcoming, genuine, and excited to share the love of Jesus with kids entering camp. Every morning during staff training, there was a set time for us to slow down and read the Word, so I started reading the book of John. But I believed the gospel was real for everyone else. It was real for the sweet Christian girls who knew Jesus and were thrilled to give away their entire summer to serve. But it couldn't apply to me—I was still trying to figure out how I ended up there and felt worlds away from Jesus. But I kept reading, and the same stories of the miracles and life of Jesus that I had grown up learning in church began to mean something different to me. I began to see myself in these stories and slowly felt the Lord gently love and pursue me.

During our staff training, we were equipped with the gospel and how to share it. But more than just learning how to share the gospel with the kids I would be working with, during our training, the gospel came alive for me. Jesus died for ME. Jesus died for MY sin and shame. And if I believe that the Father raised Him from the dead, then I am saved. I had accepted Jesus into my life at a young age, but I never truly knew how to follow Him. I never felt close to Him, and I surely wasn't steady and constant in my faith. Still, I continued to keep my guard up at staff training, but the Word and the love and acceptance of the community of believers I had found kept working at my heart.

Ephesians 2:8 says, *For by grace you have been saved through faith. And this is not your own doing, it is the gift of God, not a result of works, so that no one may boast* (ESV). That verse spoke directly to the voices in my head that told me I didn't deserve to be accepted by Jesus because I didn't have a squeaky clean record or didn't exactly live a life for His glory. It's not by works that God loves and accepts us but by grace through faith. It's not up to us to save ourselves. Instead, we need only accept that we are in need of the miraculous grace of a Savior who gave Himself up for us.

Ephesians 1:4 says, *For he chose us in him, before the foundation of the world, to be holy and blameless in love before him* (CSB). His decisions to create us and die for us were not made haphazardly. Our God is personal. The Father knew us and purposefully chose us before the foundation of the earth. As Jesus was suffering on the cross, my name crossed His mind. He knew me fully and completely—mistakes, shame, sin, and all—and He still chose to suffer for me so that He could save me. I still almost can't believe it.

As camp began, I was so nervous. It turns out that loving on kindergarteners is challenging but so beyond fun. I ended up loving my experience; that week, I witnessed many of my kids come to know Jesus and want to be saved. God used me, who had felt so far from Jesus just weeks before, to plant seeds and watch salvation unravel before my own eyes. It didn't make sense, but stories in the book of John kept reminding me that Jesus chose the unexpected as His disciples, flipped tables, and did everything the exact opposite way people thought He would.

One Sunday, our friends and I went to a local church in Dallas, Texas, where the story of Jesus healing the leper was told. Matthew 8:2-3 says, *Right away a man with leprosy came up and knelt before him, saying "Lord, if you are willing, you can make me clean." Reaching out his hand, Jesus touched him, saying, "I am willing; be made clean." Immediately his leprosy was cleansed* (CSB).

Jesus had touched the man with leprosy. In a time and age when lepers would go the rest of their lives without being able to be within six feet of any human without breaking Jewish law, Jesus touched him. In front of crowds of people, Jesus chose to touch the source of sickness directly. And He does the exact same for us. He isn't a God who chooses to sit comfortably in heaven and save us from our sin. He's a God who took the humble form of a servant and was mocked, beaten, insulted, and killed on a cross for our sins. He delights in coming directly into our messy sin and healing us with His touch and His presence.

As I sat in that church seat in Dallas, I felt the Lord's presence as keenly as the man who had been healed from leprosy.

On the car ride home to Mississippi from Texas, I spent the entire six hours talking to Jesus, crying to worship music, and begging for answers. How would I live my life now that God had wrecked it in the best way at camp? The life I had been living, my friends, the boy I was dating—none of it pointed me towards Jesus. The thought of having to leave the comfortable bubble of a strong Christian community, where living for Jesus was simple, made me uneasy. I knew I was about to step into extremely uncomfortable circumstances where I would have to make very big decisions. I was terrified, but I put my small and scared yes on the table.

In the days following, doors slammed shut. I felt led to end my relationship with a boy I had never imagined myself leaving. I let the Lord pick up the broken pieces with His Word, lots of tears, and prayer. As I sobbed, feeling the weight and fear of what laying my life down for Jesus really looked like, I opened my Bible to the book of Romans.

> *Not only that, but we rejoice in our sufferings, knowing that suffering produces endurance, and endurance produces character, and character produces hope, and hope does not put us to shame, because God's love has been poured into our hearts through the Holy Spirit who has been given to us* (Romans 5:3-5 ESV).

I read that, and I rejoiced. I let every hurtful emotion out and began, oddly enough, rejoicing and praising Jesus for all that was steady: His character. His actions. His kindness towards me. His protection. His compassion. His strength. I praised Him that, as I was in shambles, He was compassionate enough to hold me and be the steadfast rock that would heal me. As I kept rejoicing in Him, I felt the most holy and overwhelming peace wash over me, and I let Him hold me in those hard moments.

Jesus healed so many broken things over the next weeks as I kept turning to Him in the loss, growing pains, and fear. I spent more time in the Word than ever before, and when the enemy attacked and made me feel unworthy of His love, God kept speaking.

> *For I am persuaded that neither death nor life, nor angels nor rulers, nor things present nor things to come, nor powers, nor height nor depth, nor any other created thing will be able to separate us from the love of God that is in Christ Jesus our Lord* (Romans 8:38-39 CSB).

What a joy there is in the finished work of Christ. Because He sacrificed Himself and covered us, there is nothing that can separate us from the love of God in Christ.

The Lord brought me one of the biggest blessings of my life when I least expected it. I remember telling my best friends that I wouldn't date another boy for another ten years after all I had just been through. I was so content with my relationship with Jesus and had no desire to date anyone at all. At the same time, I began FaceTiming my guy friend from camp about what God was teaching us. Our simple FaceTime calls turned into him being my date for a family wedding back in Texas. We had a dreamy first date—a Bible study picnic, paddle boarding on Lake Austin, and slow-dancing under the stars. And he met my whole extended family. The funny, Texas, God-fearing boy from camp I had become best friends with ended up being my husband. Talk about a plot twist.

The girl who dreaded being a camp counselor would never imagine that two years later, she would be married to a Texas boy, finishing her senior year in college, and living a life surrendered to Jesus. The moment I lost my life as I knew it, I gained Him. It came with growing pains, and sometimes still isn't easy. Jesus tells us that to follow Him, we must lay our lives down and take up our cross. The pressing, the stretching, and the growing pains are all worth the joy of His presence and the blessings that come from walking under His protection and in His will for your life.

When I feel unworthy to sit in His presence, come to the altar, or be His friend, I am reminded that He is the same God who sat with me and pursued my heart at camp. He saw every piece of me and still chose me. He reached into the pieces of my heart I had named unlovable, and He loved me anyway. He saw me completely and still does today.

He's here to do the same for you. All He needs is your small yes.

YOU ARE NOT ALONE IN WAITING

by Lisa Tofano Hathaway and Mendez Nelson

Waiting is not fun. Nobody likes to wait. In today's world of technological advancements, things often occur rapidly, and we can jump to the conclusion that we should no longer be required to wait. In God's economy, however, things often happen at a rate different from the world's. God does not get in a hurried rush to make things happen like we do. Ecclesiastes 3:1 says it like this, *There is a time for everything, and a season for every activity under the heavens* (NIV).

God is the author of our stories. He already knows the end from the beginning. God is more concerned with our eternity, while we tend to be more carnally minded. We are not equipped to comprehend all God has planned and all He is doing behind the scenes to work for good on our behalf. But we can always choose to trust that He is with us and for us as we wait.

> *I remain confident of this: I will see the goodness of the Lord in the land of the living. Wait for the Lord; be strong and take heart and wait for the Lord* (Psalm 27:13-14 NIV).

While waiting may seem bad to us, not everything about waiting is negative. It actually strengthens our character as well as our faith. Waiting, in a biblical sense, is usually coupled with hope, which is a confident expectation of good from God. We can choose to cultivate hope as we wait on the Lord.

> *But those who hope in the Lord will renew their strength. They will soar on wings like eagles; they will run and not grow weary, they will walk and not be faint* (Isaiah 40:31 NIV).

We seem to have timelines in our minds of when things should happen. For example, many of us have picture-perfect images and scenarios in our heads of how things should look when we reach certain ages. Sadly, in our planning, we often leave God out of the equation until we need Him to hurry up and make something happen. But God desires a relationship with us that grows throughout our lifetimes. He wants us to know Him intimately. He wants to transform us into the image of his Son, who died to save us and set us free. This gradual transformation is a process called sanctification; sanctification, by definition, takes time. *It is God's will that you should be sanctified* (1 Thessalonians 4:3a NIV). God makes us pure and holy through this sanctifying process. Some people have described it as being set apart for the Lord's purposes. *But we should always give thanks to God for you, brothers and sisters beloved by the Lord, because God has chosen you from the beginning for salvation through sanctification by the Spirit and faith in the truth* (2 Thessalonians 2:13 NASB).

Patience is a fruit of the Spirit which God develops in us as we wait. God has a purpose in our waiting. It will certainly not always be easy when we wait on the Lord, but it will always be fruitful in due time. *And not only so, but we glory in tribulations also: knowing that tribulation worketh patience; and patience, experience; and experience, hope* (Romans 5:3-4 KJV.)

When Jesus was here on earth in bodily form, he encouraged us to spend time like Martha's sister Mary did, sitting at His feet. We can choose to put aside our own agendas and seek God's agenda in our times of waiting. *But seek first his kingdom and his righteousness, and all these things will be given to you as well* (Matthew 6:33 NIV).

We are never alone when we are waiting. God is with us and is doing a magnificent work in us. God sees you as you wait. Just wait and see!

. . . .

CHRISTIN BANDY

One thing about Christin Bandy is that she is very passionate about pursuing the Lord and about serving His people. She loves the local church and serving her city through local outreach.

Christin has been a follower of Christ since a very young age and has followed her calling to ministry by working full-time in college ministry at Pinelake Church. She has also served the Lord in multiple countries, such as the Dominican Republic and Canada.

Christin has a Bachelor's in Business Administration from Mississippi State University and served her sorority there as the Bible Study Chair. She enjoys doing crossfit, going on long walks, and spending time with her friends.

Christin strongly believes in the power of prayer and faith. She loves spending time with college students, guiding them how to read and understand the Bible.

She is excited to share her story with anyone who picks up this book!

Surrendering to God's Plan

by Christin Bandy

When I set my mind and heart on something, I will not stop until I get it. I am laser-focused.

When I was six years old, I followed my friend into my first gymnastics class. It was love at first sight—or love at first cartwheel. From that day on, being good at gymnastics was the most important thing to me. I told all my friends and family I was going to be in the Olympics. As I got older and had a better grip on reality, I decided that going to the Olympics would not happen, so college gymnastics would have to do.

I only went to high school for half the day so I could practice all afternoon and into the evening. I missed out on every kind of social aspect of being in high school. But I did not care. Every night, I would lie in bed and dream about doing my bar routine in a sparkly leotard, imagining a stadium filled with fans cheering for me when I landed.

My dad was a pastor, so I always knew who Jesus was and always knew the gospel. When I was 16, my youth pastor laid out what a relationship with Jesus was—trusting Him, surrendering to God, and following the Holy Spirit—and I consider that youth pastor my hero, someone who changed my life. The Lord used him as a vessel to save my soul. I was soon baptized and have been following Jesus ever since then. I often joked with my friends and family that the only things I knew anything about were gymnastics and Jesus.

Flash-forward to my senior year of high school. My dreams of college gymnastics seemed far out of reach, and I had become burned out of the sport I had dedicated my entire life to. Questions invaded my thoughts: *Do I give up? Quit?* I attended a football game at Mississippi State University; driving through campus felt a lot like heaven. But I also knew that going to school there would mean I would be choosing college without gymnastics, as the university did not have a team. So, I reasoned that couldn't be what God had for me.

May was two weeks away, and I did not have any college gymnastics offers that appealed to me. So I threw my hands up, said, "Okay!" and enrolled at Mississippi State University. When I started in the fall of 2019, I made great friends, went to a great church, and even got to coach gymnastics at a local gym.

As weeks went on, though, I began to have a full-on identity crisis.

I did not know who I was without gymnastics. I was consumed with the idea that I had failed the ONE thing I was working toward in my life. As I internalized my current reality and realized my only dream had been crushed, I became very depressed. I cried out to God every day in confusion about why He would put the passion inside me for this sport and then just take it away. I begged Him to give me another chance, another opportunity to be a college gymnast.

I think it is important to insert some hindsight wisdom here. Looking back, I know God was calling me to Mississippi State. He made it clear when I visited campus that's where the Holy Spirit was pushing me. But my identity was 90% in who I was as a gymnast and 10% in who I was as a child of God. So, when gymnastics was taken away, it felt like my whole being was dying, completely gone. I had spent much of my life thinking I was not as bad as other people because I didn't drink, party, or sleep around. However, the sin I was living in was one Jesus specifically warned against. Jesus replied: *"Love the Lord your God with all your heart and with all your soul and with all your mind. This is the first and greatest commandment"* (Matthew 22:37-38 NIV). The GREATEST commandment! 90% of my heart was loving gymnastics, which meant the other 10% was the only part loving the Lord. I had absolutely no idea how big of a deal this was and how much I would feel the consequences of this sin.

Back to the fall of 2019—my first semester of college.

About halfway through the semester, a Division 1 school in the Midwest contacted me, telling me they had an opening on their team and inviting me to join beginning that January.

I was certain my prayers had been answered! Surely, this was the Lord blessing me with everything I had always wanted. So I went. I moved my life 12 hours north and started living my dream. That was what it felt like at first, anyway. The pretty leotards, early morning lifts, and merch that identified me as a student-athlete.

What I did not know is that the next year and a half would be the most isolating period of my life—that time also bridged the gap between earth and heaven for me more than I have ever felt in my life.

I quickly realized that this university was not the same as Mississippi State. I was confused as to why no one wanted to go to church with me, and I really didn't understand the jokes about Christians that my coach openly made in front of me. I decided the Lord had sent me there to be a light and share the gospel with those lost people. So I continued on with no biblical community and no one who understood why I lived the way I did.

One night, my teammates had some friends over, and they were all drinking. I sat on the couch and socialized but didn't drink anything besides water. There was a guy there who was on the football team who started to talk about how unhealthy alcohol is for you, how he didn't drink it, and that there was no one else like him. Someone quickly yelled, "Christin doesn't drink either!"

He asked, "Why not?"

The girl who called me out answered before I could, "Because she loves Jesus."

That guy's head turned so quickly toward me, and he proceeded to stare at me like I was a unicorn. Then, completely intrigued by my existence, he said, "So you probably don't cuss, smoke, or have sex either, do you?"

"No, I don't," I answered.

He shook his head as if he could not believe what he was hearing.

I share this because THIS was the culture I was in. I was abnormal. And I had never experienced living like this before. Before then, I definitely took my godly friendships for granted. I truly did not know what I had until it was gone.

Then, everything really came crashing down. We were going to compete in a "Pride" themed competition. My coaches wanted us to wear rainbows in our hair and t-shirts that advertised our Pride support. I was a freshman who had been on this team for three months, and now I was about to tell them that I could not participate for reasons they would not understand. Thus, I was thrown into a world of complete isolation where my teammates didn't want to be friends with me. To add to my isolation, COVID-19 was about to hit, which, as we all know, made nearly all communication technology-based.

Throughout the previous four months, I consistently had quiet times with the Lord, went to church, and prayed. I wasn't consciously running away from the Lord, so I could not understand why I felt like all the life had been sucked out of me. While it was true I did not have any physical people around me who were encouraging me in my faith, I thought all I needed was God. Week after week, I would sit in church and cry, wondering why I was so unhappy. I was at the lowest point, the rockiest bottom I had ever felt, and I didn't know why.

That is when my prayer life started to change.

The first prayer I started to pray stemmed from the story of Joshua in Jericho, as told in Joshua chapter 6. The Lord told Joshua He had already delivered Jericho and instructed him to march around the city every day for six days. Then, on the seventh day, Joshua and his army were to march around the city seven times. On the seventh march on that seventh day, the walls of Jericho fell. Before the walls fell, the army had continued marching as the Lord instructed, even though it seemed as if nothing was happening. They remained faithful until the Lord delivered. So I decided I would march around my dorm building seven times while praying that God would send me a friend.

I know I probably looked crazy. I even felt a little weird, but this was the beginning of my finding out how powerful and tangible the power of God is when we pray specifically and then act. On the seventh march around my building, nothing happened. But I knew God heard the prayer I was crying out; I believed He saw me.

Soon after, I had just driven some girls on my team somewhere and pulled back into the parking lot where I lived. I sat and stared at the snow that was on the ground and thought about my life. I had everything I had ever wanted. I didn't want much, but I had it. But I felt so empty and isolated and alone. I cried and cried that night there in my car because I had no one to blame besides myself. Then, I heard a knock on my window. A girl was standing there, so I rolled down my window. "Hey, I just saw you crying, and I was wondering if you needed a hug," she said.

I kind of laughed at first, but I got out of my car and hugged her in the freezing cold because I knew that God was looking right at me and had me in His hands.

Then, as I was listening to a sermon, the pastor said, "The Lord is going to *place* you somewhere before He gives you your purpose." This statement got me thinking about where I had been placed. *Did God place me here? Or did I force this? I* could say for certain that the Lord had placed me at Mississippi State. How could I have been so blind and not seen that the Lord wanted me to stay there?

So my next prayer went as follows, "God, am I supposed to return to Mississippi State? Please show me; make it very clear to me. I am so confused about why all my dreams have come true, yet I am so broken inside."

I would pray something like this every day. Constantly.

Since I wasn't spending a lot of time with friends, the Lord became my best friend. I was constantly in communion with Him. As time went on, I felt a closeness to God I had never felt before. One day, on my drive to church, I was praying out loud; out of nowhere, I came upon a tall building I had never seen before with the word "Stark" on it—Mississippi State University is located in the city of Starkville. My heart felt like it had stopped as I read that word. The Lord had spoken to me in the closest way to being audible I have ever experienced.

Days later, I was walking to my car, about to head to practice, again in prayer, asking the Lord to confirm that I heard Him correctly. I put my phone in my purse and went into practice. When I walked out, I had a text from my roommate at Mississippi State that read, "Please come back to Mississippi State and be my roommate." My heart fell out of my chest. My former roommate and I had stayed close after I transferred; she was always very supportive of my decision to transfer so I could compete in gymnastics and had never said anything like this to me before. I knew God was speaking to me; it would almost be disobedient for me not to return to Mississippi State.

I had already signed a lease for an apartment where I was currently going to school, and there was no telling if Mississippi State would still have any of my scholarships available since I had been gone for a year and a half. But as God does, when you follow Him where He calls, He does not just leave you with the problems you created. *I am sure of this, that he who began a good work in you will carry it on to completion until the day of Jesus Christ* (Philippians 1:6 ESV). To no surprise of the Lord, I was able to get out of my lease with no problem (which is a big deal—I had signed a contract to pay them lots of money!), and I was able to receive every bit of financial aid from Mississippi State that I originally had.

As soon as I started to roll the ball with this, I felt a weight lift off my shoulders. I was able to compete that season knowing there was a light at the end of the tunnel, and I was going to make it through.

At the beginning of my college gymnastics career, I had everything the world told me I needed and could ever want. All my dreams had come true; my life was how I'd always wanted it to be at 19 years old. I am so thankful for a God who leaves the 99 for the one because what I thought I wanted my life to be does not compare to what God says my life can be.

That season of my life taught me that I do not know what is best for me. I was on a great gymnastics team, which had been my only life goal. My only one! I was 100% successful at my life goals when I was 19. But it really doesn't matter what you're doing when you are not surrounded by people who love you and are out of step with the Spirit.

Listening to where God calls you is very important. Often, when we run away from God's plan for our lives, things don't go as well as they could. I knew from the second I stepped on Mississippi State's campus the first time that THAT was my place. However, I thought the plans I had for myself were better. I tried a myriad of things to numb the pain of loneliness and isolation while living out what I thought was my dream. Every other week, I came up with a new plan to survive. I'm talking about the bare minimum of survival here. I would make plans to ensure I would wake up in the morning, get some food in me, pass my classes, and show up to practice. Every new plan failed. And the next one would fail again.

At some point, I had to give in. I had to surrender. Some of my survival plans were more detrimental than others. Since none of them included surrendering my ENTIRE life to Jesus Christ, none of them worked out. I slowly surrendered one thing after the other until all that was left was to surrender where I was placed.

God had repeated to me so many times that I had run away from where He placed me to get what I wanted. But the world does not offer what we truly and deeply long for. We can work our whole lives for something, wanting it so badly, but if our desires are not lined up with God's, we will miss out on a fully satisfying life.

I finally chose to surrender my life and say yes to wherever God called me, and I finished college at Mississippi State. When I look at my time at Mississippi State, I think about the prodigal son in Luke 15:11-32. The son ran from home to live his life the way he wanted, and when that didn't work out, he came home. And his father threw a party for him to celebrate his return. My time spent after returning to Mississippi State felt like God was throwing a party for me after returning home. It was beautiful how hard God chased me down. All He wants is for us to fall into His arms and let Him carry us. The verse I clung to after deciding to give up gymnastics, my dream life, was this: *More than that, I also consider everything to be a loss in view of the surpassing value of knowing Christ Jesus my Lord. Because of him I have suffered the loss of all things and consider them filth so that I may gain Christ* (Philippians 3:8 CSB).

After giving up gymnastics for the last time, a funny thing happened. I had no feeling of a lost identity; I didn't have a crisis of self like I did the first time I had given up my beloved sport. Instead, I fully understood that I am a child of God, and that is where my purpose rests.

Because I was obedient to go where the Lord called me, I finished my degree at Mississippi State and found my calling to ministry. I now work full-time at a church in Starkville, Mississippi.

When we surrender to the Spirit, choosing Him over ourselves, we experience things far better than anything we could ever orchestrate on our own.

The Lord saw me and had an awesome plan for my life. He sees you, too.

You Are Not Alone in Your Doubt

by Lisa Tofano Hathaway

Have you ever struggled and doubted God's goodness? Sometimes, as we go through difficulties, we wonder why God has allowed certain things to happen to us. When things go awry, it is normal for doubt to creep into our hearts and minds. We wonder, *If God is good, why is this happening?* Or we may doubt His promises to see us through our struggle or pain. But we must fight the urge to let those thoughts take control as we recognize the truth that God is always good and He will never let us down.

Doubt can enter into a relationship when we lose trust in another person. And the unfortunate part of life is that sinful people (and we are all sinful!) will let us down. People will break their promises and hurt us, both unintentionally and intentionally. When that happens, we can respond by walking away or trying to rebuild that trust by responding with a level of belief and faith in the other person and our relationship. The deeper problem comes when we carry over the mistrust from our earthly relationships and allow the darkness of humanity to color our perception of our perfect and holy God.

God longs for us to have faith in Him in all things. Even though our flesh wants us to doubt, God deserves our trust. He has never let us down. Even when we can't see His goodness, He is always operating in our best interest. There are secret things that belong to God alone. *The Lord our God has secrets known to no one. We are not accountable for them, but we and our children are accountable forever for all that he has revealed to us, so that we may obey all the terms of these instructions* (Deuteronomy 29:29 NLT).

When doubt enters our lives, it can be a bridge between our current faith and perfect faith. We continue to have our faith grown and challenged, but God is waiting for us to fully surrender to His will and know that His faith alone is perfect in our lives.

> *And Jesus answered them, "Have faith in God. Truly, I say to you, whoever says to this mountain, 'Be taken up and thrown into the sea,' and does not doubt in his heart, but believes that what he says will come to pass, it will be done for him. Therefore I tell you, whatever you ask in prayer, believe that you have received it, and it will be yours. And whenever you stand praying, forgive, if you have anything against anyone, so that your Father also who is in heaven may forgive you your trespasses* (Mark 11:22-25 ESV).

There are many people in the Bible who doubted God. But God never let them down.

Moses doubted God knew what He was talking about when He told him to lead the Israelites to the Promised Land. Moses knew what he had done in Egypt and felt the Israelites would not trust him. And he knew his own gifting, which did not include an ability to speak on behalf of God to Pharaoh. But Moses pleaded with the Lord, *"O Lord, I'm not very good with words. I never have been, and I'm not now, even though you have spoken to me. I get tongue-tied, and my words get tangled"* (Exodus 4:10 NLT).

But God knew all that information, too. It is now part of history that

Moses became a great leader. God knew exactly what He was doing, despite Moses' doubts.

Thomas was Jesus' disciple, but he doubted that Jesus was alive after the crucifixion—even though Jesus foretold of His resurrection and others had shared the good news with Thomas. Still, Thomas needed proof that Jesus was alive in order to overcome his doubts. They told him, "We have seen the Lord!" But he replied, *"I won't believe it unless I see the nail wounds in his hands, put my fingers into them, and place my hand into the wound in his side"* (John 20:25 NLT).

Jesus had a lot to do after He was resurrected! He easily could have left Thomas to wallow in his doubt, but when we watch for Him, God meets us in our doubt. Jesus intentionally showed himself to "Doubting Thomas." He let Thomas touch His hands so that Thomas could overcome his doubt.

If you are doubting God on your journey of faith, know that you are not alone. God sees you! Whether you are misplacing the hurt someone inflicted on you and allowing it to cast doubt on God like many of us do, allowing your earthly vision to cloud all that God has for you like Moses, or asking for reassurance of God's power and might like Thomas, God will meet you where you are.

God is with you in your doubt. He sees you and understands. He is patiently waiting as you come to know and trust Him more fully. He is God. He will never let you down.

. . . .

Marin Anding

Marin Anding has a big heart for Jesus and for people. She loves leading the next generation into deeper relationships with Jesus. Marin fully surrendered her life to the Lord during her freshman year of college in 2021. She is a member of Pinelake Church, where she is a worship leader, a college small group leader, and has served as a ministry intern during the summers. Marin has traveled to Uganda, Africa, twice on mission, and she would say that her heart still resides there. She has many plans to return.

Marin is a junior in college, currently working towards a degree in Business Administration, but she feels the Lord has called her to the mission field after she graduates college.

Marin loves attending concerts with friends, writing music, testing new recipes, and being in the presence of her godly community.

Marin felt she had a story to tell, and her chapter was the perfect outlet to share her story.

CONQUERED DESPERATION

By Marin Anding

I've struggled with depression and anxiety since I was about 14 years old. For the majority of my life, I have felt pretty dark and hopeless. Despite dealing with intense feelings on an ongoing basis, starting college and being in a completely different atmosphere escalated my desperation to a new level.

Stepping into my new life as a college student, I made friends way more easily than I anticipated. I also got plugged into an awesome church really early on and became involved both on campus and off campus. I checked all the boxes of what should make a young woman in college happy, and I always greeted everyone with a great big smile and warm greeting. But behind that smile, I felt like I was drowning. The joy was sucked out of everything I did.

I was miserable and couldn't seem to do anything about it. I wanted to be filled with joy so badly, but it felt so far out of reach. I've always found it easy to praise the Lord when everything is good but so hard to call out to Him when things are bad. I didn't allow anyone to sit with me in my hurt, including the Lord, thinking that since I had gotten myself to that place of desperation, it was my job to find a way out of it. I couldn't help but wonder, *Will it always be this way?*

I so wanted to be filled with the light and joy of the Lord, but there was no escaping the darkness that was overtaking my mind.

My sophomore year of college was definitely the darkest year of my life, although I'd never had more to be grateful for. At first, I was so excited to be back with all my friends and church in the place I loved so dearly. Everything was good. Then, the seasons changed, and everyone's moods, including mine, began to shift. But for me, the shift back never occurred. My anxiety climbed to an all-time high. I had panic attacks frequently. My motivation for school had disappeared. It was hard to get myself out of bed to attend class. It was hard to bring myself even to shower every day. My grades were suffering. My friendships were suffering. My ability to rest was suffering. I was suffering.

I tried so hard to cover up my pain. I didn't want to burden those who loved me the most with this heaviness. When my mom confronted me with her worries about the obvious changes in my behavior, we decided I should begin counseling; maybe that would allow me to have some mental relief. The day before my first appointment with the therapist, I felt much more down and hopeless than I had previously. For the first time in a really long time, I thought I would be better off if I weren't alive. I wasn't planning to act on it, but I was praying to the Lord to end my life because I didn't think I could suffer like that any longer. I skipped my classes that day and went for a long drive. I made it through the day and went to my small group that night. I told my small group how I had been feeling all day and allowed them to love and encourage me. I felt so much better going home that evening.

But later that night, something happened that triggered me, and I began having a terrible panic attack. For almost two hours, I felt like I was suffocating. My lungs were burning. My roommates were with me, but they couldn't understand what had happened or what they could do. Internally, I was begging for help, but I couldn't speak. I was actually scared that I was going to die. It took complete exhaustion to bring me out of it, but I was still so terrified afterward.

The next day, I skipped class and went to therapy. My mom came and stayed with me for a few days, but when she left, I was still scared to leave my house and to be alone. It took a while for my normal to be normal again.

I went to see a psychiatrist and got diagnosed with Major Depressive Disorder as well as Generalized Anxiety. I knew I had anxiety. I had panic attacks often. My heart started racing when I walked into a room full of people, the same way it did when I had to do something new for the first time alone. Knowing I had depression made me think of myself differently. How could I be a good friend, daughter, leader, servant, or employee if I was depressed? It felt like instead of a simple diagnosis, I was now holding onto a secret that no one could know. I didn't want anyone to think of me differently.

My medicine made my symptoms worse before they got better. I started having multiple panic attacks a week. I could no longer hide how I was feeling and what was going on with me because my episodes were occurring so frequently. I went to worship practice one night, thinking I would be able to make it through, but I couldn't. I had a panic attack in front of the people I was trying my best to hide it all from. I didn't want them to think I was incapable of the position they had placed me in. It broke my heart and scared me all at the same time.

Eventually, the anxiety got better. Christmas break came soon, along with rest. All the pressure of school was gone, and my schedule was empty, which was a blessing. I thought things were looking up, some of which were, but others were getting worse. The medicine helped the anxiety decline, but it increased my depression. I was putting so much time, effort, and energy into helping heal my mind, but it still felt like the world was caving in on me. It was such a discouraging time for me. I would have rather dealt with the pain I had been suffering with for so long than have it amplified and be exhausted from trying to fix it. And I was exactly that— completely and totally exhausted.

I prayed and had people pray over me for such a long time, and nothing seemed to help. I didn't doubt that God was a healer; I just doubted He wanted to heal me. I didn't really understand what healing would even look like, and that scared me. I was always deemed an emotional person. I thought being healed would strip me of my emotions, and for some reason, that terrified me, but I was so tired of hurting that I was begging God to take those feelings away or to take me away from this world because I couldn't do it anymore. There were so many days I didn't want to be alive, but I would never do something to harm myself. It felt so wrong to beg the one who gave me life to take that life from me, but it's all that I felt like I could do some days. I was at my lowest, and I didn't know what to do anymore.

The few weeks leading up to spring break were really hard for me. I was having trouble staying motivated. The joy was stripped from everything I loved. I was exhausted all the time, even when I had plenty of sleep. I was so physically, emotionally, mentally, and spiritually drained. I was planning to go to Uganda for spring break on a mission trip, but everything was getting so bad that I wasn't sure if I would even make it to the trip.

Three days before I was supposed to leave for Uganda, I felt the worst I ever had. Despite being so down all day, I attended my church's college service that night. I sat in the front row with some of my good friends. I thought I would be able to make it through the night without breaking down, but then worship started. I was so desperate to be close to the Lord and to hear His voice. The enemy's voice had gotten so loud that it had silenced the voice of the Lord. I felt so alone, and I didn't know how to turn down the enemy's voice.

During the response worship song, I was really emotional. I debated going to the altar to get prayed over, trying so hard to tell myself I was okay and talking myself out of getting prayed over. But I knew I wasn't okay, and I felt like my own prayers weren't working. I finally went to get prayed over, but I didn't feel any better after. I continued to cry through the end of the song and even a little after. A few friends noticed I wasn't doing too well. They came and talked to me, comforted me, and prayed over me. It was nice to have friends who loved me and wanted to be there for me, but I still didn't feel okay after talking with them and being prayed over by them.

One of my closest friends ended up walking me out to my car after the service. I told her that if I got in my car and drove home, I didn't think I would make it home. We were both crying at that point, and she was begging me to find hope and believe that the Lord had a purpose for my life. It was one of the hardest conversations I've ever had with someone. I had lost almost all hope. I told her she had to believe with enough strength for both of us. We were both heartbroken in that moment. I had no idea the Lord was so present then, and I still don't know how I made it home that night. I don't remember getting home.

Though I walk in the midst of trouble, you preserve my life; you stretch out your hand against the wrath of my enemies, and your right hand delivers me (Psalm 138:7 ESV).

I woke up the next morning and went to see my doctor. She asked me how I was doing, and I told her I was terrible. I told her I had almost taken my life the night before. She was seconds away from sending me to the hospital, but I told her she couldn't do that because I was leaving to go to Africa in two days. She ended up starting me on some new medication, telling me to try it and come back to see her right after spring break.

I spent the next day preparing for my trip to Uganda, getting everything packed, preparing my mind and spirit for the exhausting journey I was about to endure. I woke up Saturday, ready to go. Usually, I get really anxious as I step into something I've been anticipating for a long time. But this time, I woke up feeling like a normal human being for the first time in a long time. I didn't even notice it at first. The trip was long, exhausting, and uncomfortable. It took us almost three full days to get there, but I had the most positive spirit about it all.

Although my mind was excited, I didn't know the rigorous journey would take such a toll on my body. Who knew excitement could be so exhausting! We finally got to the compound in Uganda on Monday evening. Despite my longing to stay up talking with the other girls on my team in the next room, I was forced into recovery mode. I fell into a coma-like sleep early that evening.

The following day, we jumped into our work pretty quickly. First, we had breakfast and some quiet time to spend with the Lord, and then we set out on our morning mission. I noticed really early on in the trip that I was all in with the Lord for every second of it. I felt as if the only person who had ever brought me comfort was physically walking hand-in-hand with me every step of the way. The sudden deliverance I experienced was truly overwhelming. It's amazing what can happen when an army of believers is fighting for you. All I could do was praise God. I was filled with so much joy immediately. I may not have noticed all of the other things the Lord was doing in me at the time, but I sure did notice all He was doing around me. I got to love and be loved by people who were strangers to me. I brought hope to people who felt hopeless for so long. It felt like heaven wrapped up in five days.

My preacher and his wife were with us on the trip. I had heard his wife's story of suffering from depression for so many years and how the Lord healed her through a sermon he preached the year before. I had been yearning to have a conversation with her for so long but didn't know how to get in touch with her, and then, there she was—all the way across the world with me. I got to spend a lot of time with her on the trip. She spoke so much life into me in our short time together. We bonded quickly, and for the first time in my life, I got to have a conversation with somebody who got it.

One morning, everybody had a partner to do a morning devotional with. I did my morning devotional with the preacher's wife. There was a passage of scripture she clung to when she was walking through her hardest seasons, so we read it together. The piece of that passage that stuck out to me was Isaiah 58:9 (ESV): *"Then you shall call, and the Lord will answer; you shall cry, and he will say 'Here I am.'"* God heard every cry. He was there all along. That night, when I was afraid to go home, He was with me. He heard me and my friends call out to Him.

One night, one of our trip leaders asked a question for us to think about and answer at our debrief the next night. He wanted us to think about a distraction we had at home and one we had been having on the trip, something that was holding us back from being fully present with the Lord, with each other, or with the people we were there to serve. I immediately knew what I would talk about the next night. I spent the entire next day preparing my heart to be vulnerable and share my struggles with people I hardly knew.

The next night, we went around the circle, sharing all our happy takeaways from the day. And then it was time for us to share our distractions. I was sitting next to one of the team leaders. He went first, meaning I would have to go second. As he began talking, my eyes started brimming with tears.

Then it was my turn. I took a deep breath and started by first telling about my distraction in Uganda. Personally, I didn't have one. For me, it felt like the enemy wasn't present there. I had been all in from the moment I opened my eyes Saturday morning to leave for Uganda. I knew not everybody could say the same, but that's how I felt.

I took another deep breath, knowing that what I was about to say would be the heaviest thing I'd ever shared with a group of people.

The people sitting on either side of me noticed that I was getting a little emotional and just put their hands on me to comfort me. I told them that I had struggled with anxiety and depression since I was really young. I confided in them how bad everything had gotten right before the trip— that the voice of the enemy was so loud that it silenced God. I confessed that I thought I was going to take my life three days before we went on our trip. The enemy had done everything he could to make sure I didn't make it to Uganda because he knew how powerfully the Lord was going to move in and through me while I was there. Then, I also got to tell them how the Lord had completely turned everything around in a matter of days. We rejoiced together. *For I consider that the sufferings of this present time are not worth comparing with the glory that is to be revealed to us* (Romans 8:18 ESV). The Lord revealed just an ounce of His glory to me after such a heavy season of suffering.

So many people on our team came up to me after we finished. Most people had no idea about my struggle, and they definitely had not imagined my struggle was as heavy as I had revealed. I never let it show. It just ate me up inside for years. I had struggled alone, never letting anyone, not even the Lord, help me carry the burden.

The entire trip home, I journaled and prayed, trying to prepare myself to return to reality. I knew what I experienced in Uganda might not be permanent. I knew the peace I felt might not last. I knew that my faith would struggle and hit lows again in the future. Still, because of what I experienced in Uganda, I was ready to praise the Lord for the rest of my days for offering me a sense of relief and peace I had never experienced ever before in my life. Whether I was healed fully forever or had experienced temporary relief didn't matter.

But as for me, I will look to the Lord; I will wait for the God of my salvation; my God will hear me (Micah 7:7 ESV).

My God is good.

My God sees me. He hears me. He never leaves me nor forsakes me.

My God will stand by my side, holding my hand every step of the way—whether I can see and feel Him or not.

And my God is with you, too.

YOU ARE NOT ALONE
WHEN YOU SIN

by Lisa Tofano Hathaway and Mendez Nelson

God knew long before He created the world that His beloved children would sin. That is why He sent a Savior for us. When we accept Jesus into our hearts, God cleanses us, making us as if we have never sinned. We are forgiven. Jesus takes our sin and gives us His righteousness.

1 John 3:1 states, *See what great love the Father has lavished on us, that we should be called children of God! And that is what we are! The reason the world does not know us is that it did not know him* (NIV).

God does not leave us all alone when we face sin. He came to earth specifically to save sinners! It does not surprise God when we sin—even Jesus Himself was tempted to sin. But temptation itself is not a sin—we will always have the ability to choose our actions. So, what are we to do when we are tempted to sin? The Bible says God provides us a way out of temptation—He is always waiting for us to come to Him. When you are tempted to sin, remove yourself from the temptation and go to God in prayer. He will show you the way out and empower you to make the right choice. Focusing on God and His love for you will lessen your desire to sin willingly.

God is the author and giver of life, and He is our loving protector. In Philippians chapter 4, He tells us *to be of the same mind in the Lord* (Philippians 4:2 NIV). If our thoughts do not reflect what God tells us to think about, we may be listening to the wrong voice—possibly the voice of the enemy, others, or even our own voice. Negative thought patterns can lead us off track and into sin. The truth sets us free, but only if we know it! Jesus is the truth.

Then you will know the truth, and the truth will set you free (John 8:32 NIV).

My sheep listen to my voice; I know them, and they follow me. (John 10:27 NIV).

Here is the really good news: Even when we make the wrong choice and sin willingly, when we allow Him to, Jesus stands in our place as guilty, pronouncing us innocent by His shed blood. Only Jesus has the power to do this because He lived a sinless life and then died a sinner's death on the cross, taking the punishment for our sins.

John explains Jesus' saving grace in 1 John 2:2. *He is the atoning sacrifice for our sins, and not only for ours but also for the sins of the whole world* (NIV).

But where sin increased, grace increased all the more (Romans 5:20b NIV).

Praise the Lord, my soul; all my inmost being, praise his holy name. Praise the Lord, my soul, and forget not all his benefits— who forgives all your sins (Psalm 103:1-3a NIV).

We can and do sin by our actions, words, and thoughts. Every sin puts a divide between ourselves and God. But when we offer ourselves to Jesus, every sin, whether inward or outward, and no matter how big or small, is covered and forgiven by the blood of Jesus.

When we give our lives in submission to God, in His goodness, He will forever lead us to repent of our sins. The Holy Spirit will continually remind us that Jesus died to forgive us, taking our place and punishment. His ongoing grace and mercy cause us to rejoice in our souls as we become a sharper reflection of the holy God who created us.

When Jesus was on the cross, onlookers made fun of Him. *"He saved others,"* they said, *"but he can't save himself! He's the king of Israel! Let him come down now from the cross, and we will believe in him"* (Matthew 27:42 NIV). They accused Jesus of not being able to save Himself; they were unable to understand that as He allowed Himself to die, He was saving them. He was saving us by paying our penalty for sin, which was death, so we wouldn't have to. Jesus was dying to offer us eternal life with God.

Jesus died to save you from your life of sin. You are never alone when you sin. Your loving Savior is right beside you, paying your debt and offering you full forgiveness.

• •

Be'Be' Rayborn

Be'Be' Rayborn is a follower of Christ who cherishes her connection to the church. During her walk with Christ and His church, she has felt lavish love and grace, knowing it is the redemptive work of Jesus that makes her whole, not the world.

Originally from Mississippi, Be'Be' embarked on a modeling career that took her to various cities worldwide, including New York, London, Paris, and Norway. Despite her travels, she ultimately found solace and belonging in her home state of Mississippi.

Be'Be' holds a degree in Communication with a focus in Public Relations and a minor in Religion from Mississippi State University. She has a particular passion for aiding women affected by human trafficking.

During her college years, Be'Be' served as the president of No Longer Bound, a student-led organization dedicated to raising awareness about trafficking and supporting local victim service shelters through fundraising efforts. In addition to her advocacy work, Be'Be' enjoys the color baby pink and has a fondness for cats.

THE PRODIGAL DAUGHTER

by Be'Be' Rayborn

My name is Be'Be' Rayborn. At first glance, you might perceive me as someone who has experienced a wide array of accomplishments, spanning from high school to the culmination of my college years. Throughout this journey, I've been voted a class favorite annually, graced the homecoming court multiple times, and ventured to New York, where I modeled for esteemed brands like Maybelline and Fila. Perhaps you see my identity as the put-together sorority girl or the homecoming queen.

Despite outward appearances, throughout my life I've struggled internally, feeling unwanted and lonely. All that changed when my affections were made new in Christ through a work of the Spirit. The Lord's undeniable grace transformed my soul, shifting my life focus and purpose.

There was a time when I was unaware of how my sin intertwined with my heart. I covered up much of what was going on inside me.

In seasons that looked picture-perfect, I struggled with the heart-shattering pain of feeling unwanted and friendless. I struggled with gut-wrenching heartache that led to isolation, depression, and feelings of being unseen and alone. Loneliness and depression plagued me, exacerbated by my own choices. Often, we bask in the darkness of loneliness and pain while we grieve the loss of relationships and friendships. We make ourselves victims of our own thoughts. In my pain, I reached for immediate comfort, which led me into relationships that did not honor the Lord.

Due to extreme weight loss from my battle with depression, I graduated from high school with the "perfect model measurements." So, I went straight to New York to model for an agency I had signed with that spring.

In the city, I drifted further from the Lord, seeking solace in worldly distractions. Though I was states away from where I had grown up and the people my heart hurt over, I carried that brokenness with me every mile. I did not have the peace one has when living and abiding with the Creator of the universe. Instead, I ran from high to high. Eventually, I reluctantly returned to Mississippi State to attend college, feeling devoid of friends, academic ambition, and hope for the future.

At the beginning of my college journey, I wanted to start over. I wanted to be seen, loved, and embraced. And I let my flesh take the lead. I wanted to change, but my heart was not filled with confession and repentance. When I finally broke and stopped trying to numb my pain in the ways of the world, the Lord showed me He was rich in mercy and abundant in grace. I laid it all at the foot of the cross, and Christ captured my affections. How could I not fall in love with Christ when He first loved us? He took every shattered piece of me and didn't just put me back together but made a new creation of my heart and soul. 2 Corinthians 5:17 tells us: *Therefore, if anyone is in Christ, he is a new creation. The old has passed away; behold, the new has come* (ESV). This is true for the whole trajectory of our lives. Our hearts, once given to Christ, have new affection; our mission and purpose become greater than that of ourselves. We no longer operate in vain conceit but for the glory of Christ Jesus. We begin to seek the face of our Lord, not just as a "hail Mary," but as a way of life.

I will spend the rest of my days telling of the Lord's goodness.

This verse in Psalms is exactly my testimony. I was living in my own foolish way, afflicted with grief to the point I could barely eat, until I handed over my life to the Lord.

> *Some were fools through their sinful ways, and because of their iniquities suffered affliction; they loathed any kind of food, and they drew near to the gates of death. Then they cried to the LORD in their trouble, and he delivered them from their distress. He sent out his word and healed them, and delivered them from their destruction. Let them thank the Lord for his steadfast love, for his wondrous works to the children of man!* (Psalm 107:17-21 ESV).

Where my sin had abounded, His mercy abounded ten-fold—restoring me in ways I never deserved.

We often see people in the Bible reason over what the Lord calls them to do in obedience. The last verse in the book of Judges sums up Israel's disobedience—how they spiraled into deep darkness by following their own ways. *In those days there was no king of Israel. Everyone did what was right in his own eyes* (Judges 21:25 ESV).

We live either worshipping the Lord or bowing to our own flesh and sinful desires. You cannot serve two masters. And serving our flesh will always lead to destruction.

> *For the one who sows to his own flesh will from the flesh reap corruption, but the one who sows to the Spirit will from the Spirit reap eternal life* (Galatians 6:8 ESV).

Christianity is not a democracy where we have a decision in who God is and what His law says. It is a theocracy in which God is the King and the Leader. We do not have a say in what is or is not honoring to Him; He has laid it out in His Word for us. While the only thing we must do to be saved is to put our faith in Jesus, God does ask us to choose obedience to Him every day.

Although it is true that when we fail, we can immediately repent and turn away from our sin, the Christian life should be one of sanctification as we continually grow in holiness. If we really lay our lives at the feet of King Jesus and follow the Lord, we will grow, and our new lives will not look the same as when we lived unconvicted in the flesh. God calls us to die to our flesh and earthly desires daily.

> *Then Jesus said to His disciples, "If anyone desires to come after Me, let him deny himself, and take up his cross, and follow Me. For whoever desires to save his life will lose it, but whoever loses his life for My sake will find it"* (Matthew 16:24–26 ESV).

Reader, allow me to share with you a beautiful revelation: Dying to our flesh means changing our habits. This process can be painful to our ego, pride, and self-centered lifestyle. But oh, how worth it the discomfort is. The Creator of the cosmos, who intricately created your being and knows you better than your own flesh and blood, will take you in the care of His sovereign, mighty hand if you just willingly come to sit at His feet and lay your life in His hands.

Why would we for even a second believe that the fleeting pleasures of this world would ever fill our hearts the way the One who knit us together in our mother's wombs can fulfill our soul? When we yield to God, we gain a truth that we can so deeply rest in, even when the world around us is raging. I will not market Jesus to you and try to convince anyone their life will be "happier" if they submit. Jesus cannot be put into a box of modern-day consumerism. It is His truth and the truth that is our Lord that is so awe-strikingly magnificent that once you see the beauty and the realness of it all, how could we ever look away? When you turn to God, you will have a life rooted in a truth that will never die. *The grass withers, the flower fades, but the word of our God will stand forever* (Isaiah 40:8 ESV).

At the beginning of my college experience, I had moments of severe anxiety. I longed for the temporary relief humans offer even though I knew who the Lord was, which led me to make mistakes. I didn't speak honestly about what was going through my mind. The thoughts we suppress and grow silent about are the same thoughts the enemy uses to whisper the loudest lies. "You're too far gone." "You'll be stuck in this cycle forever." "You're too damaged for someone to ever care deeply for." Satan is the king of lies.

But our God is the Lord of truth. He wants us to praise His name.

I learned to praise the Lord's name and His promises. When we put our faith in Jesus Christ, we become a new creature and Satan is rendered powerless—he cannot stand against the Lord.

Jesus came to earth to offer us the ability to be distanced from Satan. This was planned far in advance of Jesus' birth, as evidenced in Genesis 3:15 when the Lord said to the serpent: *I will put enmity between you and the woman, and between your offspring and her offspring; he shall bruise your head, and you shall bruise his heel* (ESV). Though this may seem metaphorical, it is a direct reference to Jesus Christ coming to earth to save us from the death of our sins and being killed by Satan's seed—a non-believing people. Yet upon Jesus' resurrection, He crushed the head of Satan and became the substitutionary atonement of mankind's sins. While Satan wages war on earth, we must fight our flesh daily through the armor God tells us to put on.

Finally, be strong in the Lord and in his mighty power. Put on the full armor of God, so that you can take your stand against the devil's schemes. For our struggle is not against flesh and blood, but against the rulers, against the authorities, against the powers of this dark world and against the spiritual forces of evil in the heavenly realms. Therefore put on the full armor of God, so that when the day of evil comes, you may be able to stand your ground, and after you have done everything, to stand. Stand firm then, with the belt of truth buckled around your waist, with the breastplate of righteousness in place, and with your feet fitted with the readiness that comes from the gospel of peace. In addition to all this, take up the shield of faith, with which you can extinguish all the flaming arrows of the evil one. Take the helmet of salvation and the sword of the Spirit, which is the word of God. And pray in the Spirit on all occasions with all kinds of prayers and requests. With this in mind, be alert and always keep on praying for all the Lord's people (Ephesians 6:10-18 NIV).

During that first painful semester at college, a friend who loved the Lord reached out to me. Although Paris Baker and I had gone to high school together, we were not super close. She took me to get ice cream and asked me how I was doing; I completely broke. I cried and told her I couldn't do it anymore and I hardly had the will to live. I was so tired and lonely, so confused and sad. I had been diagnosed with depression and anxiety three years earlier, yet at that moment, I felt as if I had no more will to keep trying. Like I was drowning. She looked at me with the kindest eyes and told me the Lord loved me and that she was there for me.

I knew if I wanted to follow the Lord fully, I needed to make some changes in my life and relationships. After making some hard decisions, I sat in the silence of my car, singing praises to God.

That following day was Wednesday, the night our college ministry had service. A group of girls who were friends with Paris reached out to offer me a ride to church. I went. Feeling so unsure of my future, I walked to the altar, dropped to my knees, and wept. I wept because my heart ached for the way I had been living and for the people I had given up along the way. I was guilty, yet I was forgiven. Suddenly, I felt several pairs of hands on my back. There I was—huddled in a pile, surrounded by God-fearing college women praying over me. I began crying harder, but they were tears of relief. Relief that these girls who did not yet know me wanted to pray over me and for me. Never had I ever experienced such a beautiful thing.

These women became my best friends, who I did Bible studies with, prayed with, lived with, and broke bread with. In fact, that very night after church, they asked me to live with them the following year. They had signed for a five-bedroom apartment even though there were only four of them and were unsure who would fill the vacancy. My only other option had been to live in sorority housing, but I had not yet made any close friends in my pledge class.

It has now been almost two years since that night, and I still live with some of the same girls who became my best friends on that night when I needed them most. It was such a God moment; glory be to Him.

We are not called to walk this journey alone. God calls us to be the BODY of Christ, praying for and encouraging each other. If you are not part of a God-fearing community, stop reading and pray. Pray for the Lord to lead you to which church He wants you to be a part of, guiding you to a Christ-centered community. *Do not be anxious about anything, but in everything by prayer and supplication with thanksgiving let your requests be made known to God* (Philippians 4:6 ESV). Through our prayers, we have power against the enemy. Even when we fail for words, we can trust the Holy Spirit is praying for us. *Likewise the Spirit helps us in our weakness. For we do not know what to pray for as we ought, but the Spirit himself intercedes for us with groanings too deep for words* (Romans 8:26 ESV).

Throughout the next year, I prayed the Lord would put me where He wanted me. I started attending and, for the first time, became a member of a church. Being with the body of Christ at Grace Church has been so edifying. I will forever be grateful for Christ and His bride, the church.

I've learned that loneliness can hit us in so many different circumstances as the enemy tells us that we are not loved or wanted. But this is a lie. God is always waiting to tell you that you are everything to Him.

You are loved.

Being the new person in a new place is hard and can make you feel like there is no place for you.

Social media and cliques can seem perfect, but often are not what they seem. And the wrong clique can lead you down a path of disobedience for quick pleasure that will only end up in deeper emptiness.

Breaking up with someone can leave you feeling damaged and unwanted.

When you feel alone and unseen, pray. Pray without ceasing. Pray for a

God-fearing community, Christian friends to surround you, and for the Lord to guide your steps. And as you pray, know that you are not alone—the Creator of the universe is walking beside you, longing for you to lean on Him.

There is nothing you can do that can make God turn away from you. He is beside you, waiting to offer you His grace. If you are in a season where you feel guilt or shame, offer yourself to Christ and accept His forgiveness. Confess and turn back to the loving Savior who will make you whole.

God will never let you down. If you put your trust and hope for affection in humans, you will deflate when those relationships crumble. But there will always be grace and restoration through a life with Christ.

As I grew, I began to understand that when my thoughts were wrapped up in what could make my feeble human heart happy, it always ended in pain and confusion.

And we know that the Lord is not a God of confusion.

Our Lord is El Roi—the God who sees us. He sees us in our pain. He sees us in moments of selfishness, weakness, and fear. And yet, He is slow to anger and steadfast in love. That is who our God is.

Our feelings and reasoning do not dictate the character of God. Knowing who He is and focusing on His characteristics allows us to take every thought captive. When we base the image of God on our circumstances and feelings, it can lead us to become despondent or depressed. Our holy and perfect God is unchanging and good. He is just. He sees the broken-hearted and afflicted. He yearns for us to cast our cares on Him. He is a jealous God and wants your whole heart and life—not some of it. The Creator loves His creation. He sent His Son, that through His death and resurrection, we may live in unity with Him and never perish but have eternal life.

We will all have to face loneliness. We will all have moments when our hearts feel empty. Know that God is there waiting to meet you where you are. In those moments when you feel separated from God, make the decision to pray and cry out to Him anyway. In your loneliness, take the time to examine who you truly are. You are a child of God.

The Lord saved me. There is a very real enemy that wants you to believe you are alone. But there is also a very real God who saves and embraces those who turn to Him.

Jesus declared... "Come to me, all you who are weary and burdened, and I will give you rest. Take my yoke upon you and learn from me, for I am gentle and humble in heart, and you will find rest for your souls. For my yoke is easy and my burden is light." (Matthew 11:25, 28-30 ESV).

YOU ARE NOT ALONE EVER

by Mendez Nelson

I Most likely, we are each privately wrestling with something deep down on the inside right now. We may be facing extremely difficult circumstances and are left wondering, *Why is this happening? Where is God? Why is He allowing this into my life?* Or maybe we are experiencing guilt or wondering if we could have done something differently in a given circumstance. When we wrestle with these kinds of thoughts privately, we can be left feeling unseen and alone. But you are not alone. The apostle Paul wrote about some of his inner wrestlings in Romans.

> *I do not understand what I do. For what I want to do I do not do, but what I hate I do. And if I do what I do not want to do, I agree that the law is good. As it is, it is no longer I myself who do it, but it is sin living in me. For I know that good itself does not dwell in me, that is, in my sinful nature. For I have the desire to do what is good, but I cannot carry it out. For I do not do the good I want to do, but the evil I do not want to do—this I keep on doing. Now if I do what I do not want to do, it is no longer I who do it, but it is sin living in me that does it. So I find this law at work: Although I want to do good, evil is right there with me. For in my inner being I delight in God's law; but I see another law at work in me, waging war against the law of my mind and making me a prisoner of the law of sin at work within me. What a wretched man I am! Who will rescue me from this body that is subject to death? Thanks be to God, who delivers me through Jesus Christ our Lord!* (Romans 7:15-25a NIV).

No matter who we are, what we've done, or what has been said to us or about us, God is still with us. He does not and will not leave us even when we feel we deserve Him to leave. *Then they cried out to the Lord in their trouble, and he delivered them from their distress* (Psalm 107:6 NIV).

The truth is God assures us in His Word that He is always with us. No matter what trouble we are in, He will be with us and will deliver us. When we are in seasons when God seems silent, we must choose to trust His promises no matter what we see or feel. We can learn to *walk by faith, not by sight* (2 Corinthians 5:7 NKJV). This means we trust what God says to be true over what we see or feel.

He proclaims to us in His Word, *"I will never leave you nor forsake you"* (Hebrews 13:5b ESV). This promise can be difficult for us to believe and accept due to our tendency to judge God by human standards. People who are supposed to love us can disappoint us by leaving us, and we can project our hurts from being abandoned onto God.

> *The Lord is good, a refuge in times of trouble. He cares for those who trust in him* (Nahum 1:7 NIV).

It is easy to become overwhelmed with despair when hard times come upon us unexpectedly. We may even begin to doubt God's love or His existence. We tend to judge Him based on our circumstances. If things are going well, God must be good; if our circumstances are difficult, it can be tempting to believe God is bad. But our God is always good! He never changes even when our situations do. And furthermore, His love for us never changes.

This is what the Lord says... "Do not fear, for I have redeemed you; I have summoned you by name; you are mine. When you pass through the waters, I will be with you; and when you pass through the rivers, they will not sweep over you. When you walk through the fire, you will not be burned; the flames will not set you ablaze. For I am the Lord your God, the Holy One of Israel, your Savior." (Isaiah 43:1-3a NIV).

We are never alone. Ever. God is always with us. His name is Immanuel, which literally means "God is with us." As written by Matthew, Jesus' birth fulfilled Isaiah's prophecy, which stated, *"The virgin will conceive and give birth to a son, and they will call him Immanuel" (which means "God with us")* (Matthew 1:23 NIV). God's very nature and purpose for creating us was so He could be with us. Jesus left heaven to live on earth to reside in our presence physically. Then He died and rose again so God could live inside each of us in the form of the Holy Spirit when we come to believe in Him.

Our mighty, triune, holy God is here to stay. Know that you are never alone. Ever!

. . . .

AFTERWORD

Thank you for taking the time to read the stories and encouraging devotions we have shared in this book. Stepping out in obedience to write has truly been a labor of love. You, dear reader, have been prayed for. Our desire is that God has used this book to bless you no matter where you are in your life's journey. As contributing authors, we hope you have gained comfort in knowing you are not alone, especially when you experience feelings of disconnection, isolation, and loneliness.

There are four important things we hope you always remember from this book:

- **You are not invisible.**
- **You are always seen by God.**
- **You are never alone.**
- **You are significant to God.**

We also hope this book helped answer some subconscious questions you may have had, like:

- If we are wired for connection, why does it seem so far out of reach?
- Why does everyone else's life appear to be perfect?
- Why do we feel as if we often go unnoticed?
- Why do our circumstances cause us to feel overlooked and insignificant?

Our lives will continually change. But our God is steadfast; He will never change. And you are significant to Him! He sees you. He pursues you! In fact, our loving heavenly Father, the Good Shepherd, will leave the other ninety-nine sheep to search for the one sheep who has gone astray. *"And when he finds it, he joyfully puts it on his shoulders and goes home. Then he calls his friends and neighbors together and says, 'Rejoice with me; I have found my lost sheep.'"* (Luke 15:5-6 NIV).

All the authors of this book have openly shared their struggles of feeling isolated and unnoticed. Thankfully, God helped each one of them overcome their obstacles and find the one thing that truly matters—Him. He is ready and willing to do the same for you. The truth of God's Word sheds light that dispels the lies of the darkness we have believed for far too long. The truth is we are always seen by God, even when we are unnoticed by the world. In Him, we are never alone!

By God's design, we all need love, acceptance, and community. Only in Him are we able to truly find those things. Fear of rejection can hinder us from seeking community. But God does not want us to live our lives in fear of all He has created us for. *For God has not given us a spirit of fear, but of power and of love and of a sound mind* (2 Timothy 1:7 NKJV).

God loves us so much that He gives us the power to overcome what the world throws at us. We overcome only by our faith in Him. If you do not yet know Jesus as your Savior, here is a scripture you need to hear—one that will change your life if you let it:

> *If you declare with your mouth, "Jesus is Lord," and believe in your heart that God raised him from the dead, you will be saved. For it is with your heart that you believe and are justified, and it is with your mouth that you profess your faith and are saved* (Romans 10:9-10 NIV).

We can rejoice and be thankful every day of our lives because God is present with us. Always. He never leaves us or takes His eyes off of us. The Holy Spirit helps us and guides us to draw closer to Him. It is so exciting to know that the God who created the universe sees us, loves us, and calls us by name.

You are never alone. Ever.

"You are the God who sees me" (Genesis 16:13 NIV).

MORE WPP ANTHOLOGIES!

The stories shared in *Hope Alive: Debilitated to Exhilarated* are beautiful examples of how trust in God can transform our lives into a living testimony of His goodness and faithfulness. God is always with us, turning our struggles into victories and our tears into hope.

The authors of *Miracle Mindset: Finding Hope in the Chaos*, have experienced the wonders of God's provision, protection, and guidance. These stories and teachings will ignite a spark within you, propelling you to encounter the marvel of God's miracles, even in the chaos.

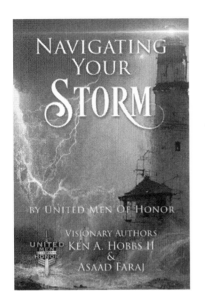

Life is full of storms and rough waters. The stories in *Navigating Your Storm: By United Men of Honor* will give you the ability to see the light of God and navigate your storm victoriously.

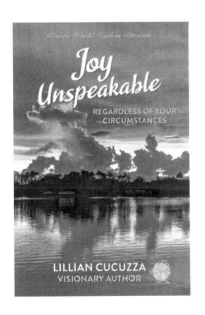

With *Joy Unspeakable: Regardless of Your Circumstances,* you will learn how joy and sorrow can dance together during adversity. The words in this book will encourage, inspire, motivate, and give you hope, joy, and peace.

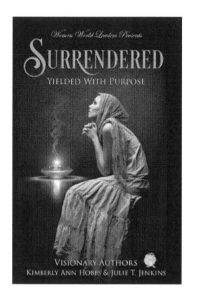

Surrendered: Yielded With Purpose will help you recognize with awe that surrendering to God is far more effective than striving alone. When we let go of our own attempts to earn God's favor and rely on Jesus Christ, we receive a deeper intimacy with Him and a greater power to serve Him.

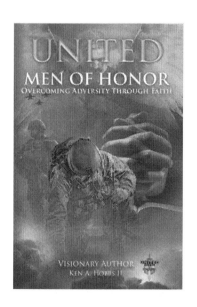

United Men of Honor: Overcoming Adversity Through Faith will help you armor up, become fit to fight, and move forward with what it takes to be an honorable leader. Over twenty authors in this book share their accounts of God's provision, care, and power as they proclaim His Word.

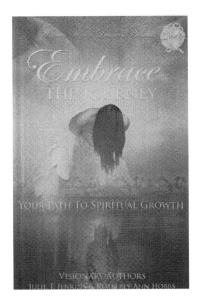

Embrace the Journey: Your Path to Spiritual Growth will strengthen and empower you to step boldly in faith. These stories, along with expertly placed expositional teachings will remind you that no matter what we encounter, we can always look to God, trusting HIS provision, strength, and direction.

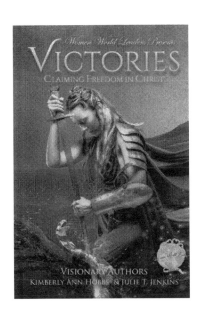

Victories: Claiming Freedom in Christ presents expository teaching coupled with individual stories that testify to battles conquered victoriously through the power of Jesus Christ. The words in this book will motivate and inspire you and give you hope as God awakens you to your victory!

WPP's Mission

World Publishing and Productions was birthed in obedience to God's call. Our mission is to empower writers to walk in their God-given purpose as they share their God story with the world. We offer one-on-one coaching and a complete publishing experience. To find out more about how we can help you become a published author or to purchase books written to share God's glory, please visit: **worldpublishingandproductions.com**

Heartbeat of a Survivor tells the story of Nita Tin, a Buddhist born and raised in an opulent lifestyle in Burma. As her country came under the control of a ruthless military dictator, Nita's whole life changed. Forced to flee her home, her soul was soon set free in a greater way than she ever dreamed possible.

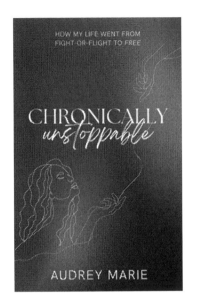

At seventeen, Audrey Marie experienced a sudden and relentless excruciating firestorm of pain. *Chronically Unstoppable* tells of her true-life journey as she faced pain, developed strength, and battled forward with hope.

The world has become a place where we don't have a millisecond to think for ourselves, often leaving us feeling lost or overwhelmed. That is why Max Gold wrote *Planestorming!*—a straightforward guide to help you evaluate and change your life for the better. It's time to get to work and make the rest of your life the BEST of your life.

Made in the USA
Columbia, SC
15 June 2024